# Loco Motion

## Physics Models for the Classroom

### Ed Sobey

Zephyr Press

Chicago

**Library of Congress Cataloging-in-Publication Data**

Sobey, Edwin J. C., 1948-

  Loco-motion : physics models for the classroom / Ed Sobey.

    p. cm.

  Includes bibliographical references.

1.  Physics—Study and teaching (Elementary)—Activity programs. 2.  Motion—

Experiments.  I. Title: Locomotion. II. Title.

  QC33.S674 2005

  372.35—dc22                                      2004028137

Cover and interior design: Rattray Design

Interior photos: Ed Sobey

© 2005 by Ed Sobey

All rights reserved

Published by Zephyr Press

An imprint of Chicago Review Press, Incorporated

814 North Franklin Street

Chicago, Illinois 60610

ISBN 1-56976-193-0

Printed in the United States of America

*To Dad,*
*who fueled my interest in building things*
*and making them go.*

# Contents

# Introduction

Fling a boomerang, race a balloon-powered car, or launch a potato across the yard—these activities are some of the pleasures of projects featured in *Loco-Motion*. Kids will work together to make and test nifty models that spin, fly, launch, or zoom across the floor.

Kids will love building and testing these kinetic models. Not only will they have tons of fun building them and playing with them, they will also take pride in having created fun toys. In this day of virtual everything, *Loco-Motion* provides activities in which kids can make real things and, in the process, learn science. Furthermore, through building, kids develop the skills and self-confidence required to undertake other projects of their own design.

The fun comes in when kids make objects that move. Once they see the promise of a kinetic toy, they commit themselves to building one. With self-satisfaction and pride they test their toy and show it to friends and parents.

The fun expands as *Loco-Motion* builders try to make their models roll farther, fly higher, or go faster. Each success propels them to try something new. They create new designs and test them, learning the physics of motion and the skills of construction while having a blast. And they enjoy having the opportunity to express their creative ideas by modifying the toys to their own tastes.

For each project in the book, teachers establish the challenges and work with teams of students to make the most of specific learning opportunities. Students are toy inventors striving to make toys that meet the challenges set by teachers. They document their designs and innovations, and record test results on the inventor log pages provided with the activities.

Since launching the program Kids Invent Toys (http://www.kidsinvent.org) in 1997, I have developed a portfolio of designs for toys that kids can make quickly out of inexpensive materials. *Loco-Motion* is the collection of these activities.

The beauty of these designs is that once kids (and families) make one of the toys, they want to make more. Thus, the learning, like the vehicles in *Loco-Motion,* is self-propelling.

The allure of these activities is magical. When I demonstrate the building of kinetic toys in public museums, people crowd around to watch. I have introduced these activities to the public at leading science centers (The Tech Museum of Innovation, San Jose; Oregon Museum of Science and Industry, Portland; Pacific Science Center, Seattle; the Carnegie Science Center, Pittsburgh; and others). In every case, my workshop on making these *Loco-Motion* toys became the museum's center of attention, outdrawing their many interactive exhibits and activities. Everyone enjoys seeing and making toys.

Teachers, homeschool parents, and educators at science centers and children's museums love these activities because they engage kids and help them to learn. Most importantly, kids learn they can create things with simple materials. They also learn about the physics of motion, air pressure, gravity, electric circuits, and more.

Although *Loco-Motion* presents many new building activities, the learning approach is time-tested. Many of the greatest inventors learned science and engineering by playing with interesting materials and making toys and other devices. Tinkering and asking questions are the essence of good learning. *Loco-Motion* can transform the classroom or homeschool environment into an inventing laboratory where every student is inspired to learn.

# Getting Started

## Design, Build, Test, and Innovate

You and your students will go loco designing, building, and testing the model cars, boats, planes, and rockets described in *Loco-Motion*. The energy and interest your students show will remind you that learning can be a lot of fun.

In *Loco-Motion* projects, students design, build, and test vehicles under the specifications you give, with clear but open-ended goals. Many of the projects require students to gather measurements and allow student teams to collect, graph, and analyze data. In other words, *Loco-Motion* projects encourage students to apply science and engineering skills.

Students rarely get to experience science in action (that is, science as a verb). Almost always, it is presented as a noun—a body of facts that students need to master in order to pass tests. Science as a noun is boring and often useless. It often counters innate understandings of how the world operates and creates a second and artificial set of understandings rather than replacing inaccurate understandings. At the end of "noun science" lessons, students are ready to stop and do something different. They don't want to learn more science. Just the opposite occurs in "verb science" lessons.

Students don't want to end verb science lessons; they want to work longer on their projects even if that means cutting breaks short or continuing at home. Instead of dreading studying more information, they beg for more: they want to know how to make their models work better. Behavioral problems vanish (or at least greatly decline) and interest rises. *Loco-Motion* is verb science at its best.

*Loco-Motion* is more than a collection of fun projects to integrate into an existing curriculum. It models an ideal way of teaching and learning physical science in which students engage in self-directed inquiry, learn in their own way (intelligence style), and construct their own understanding from their experiences. Peer-to-peer learning takes place, freeing the teacher to focus on emphasizing critical concepts and correcting native misunderstandings—the misconceptions kids have about how nature or science works.

In *Loco-Motion* classrooms, the teacher takes on the role of director of research and development for a toy design company. The director assigns design challenges, provides resources and encouragement, and monitors results. Rather than providing information, the director helps teams by framing questions to spur their thinking and by ensuring that the teams are observing what is really happening.

The role of the teacher as project director continues as teachers take advantage of learning moments to foster understanding, introduce science vocabulary, and suggest additional experiments and alternative learning opportunities.

In this toy-inventing process, teams are free to make mistakes, innovate, observe other teams' designs, and help each other. They can undertake new research and, with the teacher's approval, explore creative solutions to problems. The students work as inventing teams trying to create new toys for a company.

To learn more about this "inventing to learn" process and to understand how and why it works, please check out *Inventing Toys: Kids Having Fun Learning Science* (Zephyr, 2002).

In Independence, Oregon, teachers learn how to make planes and cars in a *Loco-Motion* workshop.

## Tools and Materials

Each project has a materials list with suggested vendors. Costs for materials are quite low, making projects financially viable both for the teacher and for kids who want to continue the projects at home. Many of the materials show up in several projects, which means you can buy supplies in bulk if needed.

Restaurant supply stores are sources for straws, plates, cups, and sometimes balloons. I suggest Woodworks (http://www.craftparts.com) as a source for wooden wheels and dowels, but check the Internet for other companies. Retail outlets charge excessively for motors, wires, and batteries, so search the Internet for better deals. I often use Kelvin (http://www.kelvin.com) for propellers, motors, and clip leads. Kelvin also offers an alternative to wooden wheels: inexpensive plastic wheels. These attach to ⅛-inch dowels, which fit through standard straws to act as bearings.

Many of the raw materials for building vehicles can come from recycling bins. Cardboard, cereal boxes, two-liter soda bottles, and half-gallon and quart milk or juice containers provide the framework for many models. Masking tape and hot glue connect components in many models.

In general, projects require:

¼″ dowels for axles and spindles
Wooden wheels with ¼″ center holes or plastic wheels and 1/8" dowels
Cardboard or other recycled containers for frames and bodies
Fat straws for bearings (¼″ dowels fit through them)
Alligator clip leads to make electrical connections
9 V transistor batteries
Electric motors (inexpensive direct current "toy motors")

Most kids don't get opportunities to work with real tools, so they don't know how to use them. In *Loco-Motion* kids are encouraged to cut wood with saws, use glue guns, and use pliers. Although this practice has generated a few scrapes and sores, I haven't called an ambulance yet.

I carry a Swiss Army knife and use it repeatedly during each project. The Phillips screwdriver on a Swiss Army knife fits more screws than any other driver I've found. Surprisingly, the other tools on the knife (magnifying lens, tweezers, scissors, knife blades, and awl) are quite useful too. Also, I use a survival tool that features pliers and other blades (found at a camping or hardware store) for these projects. I use the cutting edge in the pliers to cut small dowels. Although kids are encouraged to use certain tools for these projects, do not loan them either your survival tool or Swiss Army knife.

Other tools required for these projects are hot glue guns, saws (coping, hack, and wood), measuring tape and square, clamps, vice grips, screwdrivers, and jeweler's screwdrivers. A soldering iron and dremel tool are sometimes helpful, but not required and not for student use.

## How to Use the Handouts

*Loco-Motion* provides a set of student instructions for each activity. I encourage you to reproduce these, distribute them to the class, and collect them for your assessment at the end of the activity.

The instructions are divided into four or five sections:

Design
Build (Instructions for Inventors)
Test
Reflect
Extend (not all activities include extensions)

I suggest that you distribute these handouts section by section—that is, don't give out all the instructions at one time, but provide them as each team or individual is ready for the next step. This gives you greater control over the quality and timing of the students' progress and prevents students from being overwhelmed with papers.

Following the instructions laid out in the Design sections, teams consider what their *Loco-Motion* vehicle will look like and sketch it in the space available. As much as kids like to draw, many dislike sketching their designs. These students may prefer to design by manipulating the component parts. In showing their preference (by how they attack a problem) they are indicating their preferred mode of thinking.

Directing students to sketch a design forces them to think in ways that are less comfortable and, hopefully, allows them to become more comfortable with two-dimensional representation. Sketching also fosters full team involvement: as one team member sketches, others can offer suggestions or at least understand how the vehicle will look and operate. Sketches provide a focal point for discussion and verbal thinking—another mode of thinking and learning (in addition to visualization and hands-on manipulation) engaged in this inventing process.

Young students may not be able to sketch or design their projects until you have shown them a prototype that you've assembled. Sharing your design with the class can accelerate the design process, but it usually results in every model looking similar to the one you made, so don't share unless students are struggling.

Once a team has a design in mind or on paper, give them the Build instructions. These instructions may cause them to redesign their vehicle. Have them note the design changes on their sketch (in a different color pen) or have them sketch the final design and compare it to the initial sketch design.

I provide fewer detailed instructions for the Build sections in projects presented later in the book. As students learn to think for themselves and depend less on exact directions, they will be better equipped to figure out how to make the models. Although the paucity of instructions may frustrate some, it will foster more creative approaches and provide a greater sense of joy upon a project's completion.

The Test sections outline one or more experiments to try. This is hands-on, inquiry-based science. Keep the testing going for as long as you can and encourage teams to come up with new experiments to run.

The Extend sections suggest other experiments or variations of the design challenge to try. Teams that complete the basic challenge can move on to try these extensions.

## Safety First

Working with tools can lead to minor mishaps, so stock your classroom with a few bandages. Other than bruises, scrapes, and an occasional cut or pinch, your students shouldn't experience injuries with these projects. Here are a few safety tips for kids to follow to prevent injuries:

1. Wear safety glasses! Your eyes are worth the investment of a few bucks.
2. Leave the hammer hanging on the wall. Avoid the temptation to force parts to come together or separate, or to teach an inanimate object a thing or two.
3. Watch where you point sharp tools, because they tend to move in the direction you've pointed. Extending a screwdriver toward a hand might succeed in uniting the two.
4. Look twice before cutting. Check underneath the thing you're cutting to ensure that it's the project material you're cutting and not the table. Recheck the measurement before cutting.
5. Don't exceed the pressure ratings. "If it flies well with 40 psi, how well will it fly at 80 psi?" Although I applaud the scientific questioning (and always ask such questions myself), follow common sense and don't push materials beyond their limits.
6. Don't aim kinetic models at people, animals, or other important objects. Some of the projects described here involve launching rockets. Launch only safe models, and think before you launch.
7. Avoid using household electricity to power projects. Use batteries instead.

## Science Learning

Science concept content for *Loco-Motion* activities:

| Activity | Scientific inquiry | Properties of material | Position, motion | Forces | Light, heat, electricity | Models | Computation | Energy/energy transfer | Design and systems | Nature of science |
|---|---|---|---|---|---|---|---|---|---|---|
| Gravity-powered car | • | • | • | • |   | • | • | • | • | • |
| Balloon racer | • | • | • | • |   | • |   | • | • | • |
| Propeller-drive electric car | • | • | • | • | • | • | • | • | • | • |
| Direct-drive electric car | • | • | • | • | • | • | • | • | • | • |
| Belt-drive electric car | • | • | • | • | • | • | • | • | • | • |
| Hovercraft |   | • | • | • |   | • |   |   |   |   |
| Top | • | • | • | • |   |   | • | • | • | • |
| Rocket car | • | • | • | • |   | • |   | • | • | • |
| Rubber band racer | • | • | • | • |   | • | • | • | • | • |
| Mousetrap car | • | • | • | • |   | • |   | • | • | • |
| Springer |   | • | • | • |   |   |   |   |   |   |
| Electric jitter critter |   | • | • | • | • | • |   | • | • |   |
| Gravity ball launcher | • |   | • | • |   |   | • | • |   | • |
| Flying saucer | • | • | • | • |   | • |   | • |   | • |
| Catapult | • | • | • | • |   | • | • | • | • | • |
| Trebuchet | • | • | • | • |   | • | • | • | • | • |
| Straw rocket | • |   | • | • |   | • |   | • |   | • |
| Pneumatic blast rocket | • | • | • | • |   | • | • | • | • | • |
| Fling-a-spud |   |   | • | • |   |   |   | • |   |   |
| Dynamic ping-pong ball launcher |   | • | • | • |   |   |   | • |   |   |
| Boomerang |   | • | • | • |   |   |   | • | • | • |
| Pressure rocket launcher | • | • | • | • |   | • | • | • | • | • |
| Chemical minirocket |   | • | • | • |   | • |   | • |   |   |
| Gravity-powered boat | • |   | • | • |   |   |   | • |   | • |
| Electric boat | • | • | • | • | • | • | • | • | • | • |
| Swamp boat | • | • | • | • | • | • | • | • | • | • |
| Rubber band–powered boat | • | • | • | • |   | • | • | • | • | • |
| Diving submarine |   | • | • | • |   | • |   |   |   |   |

## Entering Science Fairs and Other Competitions

Many of the models can be used as science fair projects. Students can make and test these models to discover topics that interest them. I suggest you use these models to introduce an upcoming science fair and give students a jump start on finding projects that appeal to them.

The first step in preparing for science fairs is often to send students to the library to conduct research. This strategy typically leads to bad projects as there are few topics that kids can research in the library that they can later test with reasonable experiments. Volcanoes and the solar system are common research topics that defy an elementary school student's ability to design an experiment and collect data.

Instead, start students thinking about the science fair by having them build models. As they build, they may generate ideas for projects that interest them and that allow them to conduct experiments.

As students consider possible topics, help them recognize that they need to collect, analyze, and display (graph) data from the models they build. Help them frame questions that they can answer through experimentation. Your guidance early in the process will make it much easier for them to get excited about entering the fair.

# On the Ground

Kids love to play with cars, tops, and other models, so there is no shortage of enthusiasm for these projects. The activities are structured to utilize the enthusiasm of students as they learn about science through attempting to optimize their vehicles.

These models expose kids to a variety of energy storage devices and sources. Most provide opportunities for students to take measurements and collect data. All are fun.

To add writing components to these activities, have students research relevant inventors and prepare reports. Here are some suggestions:

Karl Benz, inventor of the gasoline engine

Joshua Cowen, inventor of Lionel Trains

Gottlieb Daimler, another inventor of the gasoline engine

Rudolf Diesel, inventor of the diesel engine

A. C. Gilbert, manufacturer of American Flyer Trains and inventor of other toys

Elliot Handler, creator of Hot Wheels and cofounder of Mattel

Richard James, inventor of the Slinky

Antonio Pasin, inventor of the Radio Flyer

Nicolaus Otto, inventor of the internal combustion engine

Nikola Tesla, inventor of the induction motor

Several of these inventors have been inducted into the National Inventors Hall of Fame (http://www.invent.org) and several of the toys have been inducted into the National Toy Hall of Fame (http://www.strongmuseum.org/NTHoF/NTHoF.html).

# Gravity-Powered Car

## Challenge

Design and build a model car that can roll as far as possible across a floor, propelled solely by rolling down an inclined ramp.

## Overview

Although conceptually simple, gravity-powered cars are engaging projects. Students enjoy making and testing them, and they learn the construction techniques required for the more complex vehicles that follow. Gravity-powered cars are ideal for teaching the methods of science, which include independent research, data collection, graphing, and interpretation of graphs and data. I suggest specific materials to use, but a wide variety of materials, some free and most inexpensive, will work.

## Materials

Cardboard (1 large box or 2 small boxes)
Fat straws (1–2 per team)
¼″ dowels (budget 8″ per team)
Wooden wheels (4 per team) or plastic wheels with ⅛″ dowels and
  regular straw
Hot glue or masking tape
Sandpaper or sanding blocks (1 per two teams)
Inclined ramp
Meter sticks (2–3)

CDs make great plastic wheels if you have plastic inserts to fit inside the center hole. The inserts fit a ¼-inch dowel. Since these are much larger than the other wheels, cars using them can roll easily. The Web site www.Kelvin.com sells plastic inserts, and your postal carrier probably delivers free CDs, such as those offering Internet services.

A pine board with one-inch by four-inch sideboards (to keep cars from falling off the edge) makes a great ramp. To reduce the gap between the ramp and floor, plane or rasp wood off the bottom edge of the ramp. Cardboard, reinforced with strips of cardboard, also works. Prop up one end of the ramp with a chair or table and secure it with duct tape to prevent movement.

## Design Concept

Attach sections of straw to the bottom of the chassis (made from a rectangular piece of cardboard). Run dowels through the straws and outfit the dowels with two wheels each. Students can also try the more challenging design of three-wheeled cars.

## The Details

Ask students to choose their own teams, each with a maximum of three kids.

Cut a rectangle about four-inches by six-inches from a piece of corrugated cardboard. (This chassis needs to be small enough to fit on the ramp.) Cut two sections of straw as long as the chassis is wide. Tape or glue them to the bottom carefully, making sure they're parallel to each other. Start by aligning the chassis with a square or the edge of the worktable. Eyeball the perpendicular direction by looking at the perpendicular edge of the table or square. Glue the first straw in place.

To make sure the second straw is parallel to the first, make a jig (a device that holds component parts in their correct position) that is as wide as the distance you want between the two straws. A two-by-four-inch piece of lumber would work. Align one side of the two-by-four with the glued straw, and glue the second straw aligned with the other edge of the board.

Cut two dowels three-quarters of an inch longer that the length of the straw bearings. Sand the cut ends and attach one wheel. In most cases the dowel will make a tight fit with the wheel and you won't need (or want) to glue it. Then slide the axles through the bearings and attach the other wheels.

Straws are taped or secured with hot glue to the bottom of the chassis to make cars. Dowels fit through the straws and serve as axles to hold the wheels in place.

If the axles don't fit the wheels, you'll need to do some adjusting. If the axles are too big (in diameter), try sharpening the ends in a pencil sharpener and jamming them through the wheel opening. Once the wheel is centered on the axle, add a drop of hot glue to hold it in place.

If the axles are too small for the wheels—a common problem if you're substituting CDs for wooden wheels—you can add an insert or attachment to the wheel. Use lids from milk cartons or small wooden wheels to hold the axles. Then tape the lids or small wheels to the CD. Spin the axle to see if it is centered and adjust as necessary. Once it is centered, use a felt tip pen to draw a circle around the small wheel to guide you when you glue it. Hot glue doesn't hold well to the CDs; try using a general purpose glue instead.

## Getting Started

Let students discover how to design and build the cars to the greatest extent possible. It can be helpful, however, to show them how the straws act as bearings for the dowels. Suggest that they attach straws to the bottom of the car chassis (with glue or tape) to secure the sections of dowel that serve as axles. The wooden wheels slide snugly onto the axles.

## Teachable Moments

Once students undertake this project, your role is to help them understand the science of what's happening by asking questions. I am always amazed that students cannot answer the most basic questions about the experiment, such as "What did the car do?" Until they understand that you will hold them responsible for looking, listening, and understanding, they will take the easy way out: "I don't know."

If they say they didn't see what happened, direct them to run the experiment again with the forewarning that you will ask the same question immediately afterward. This sharpens their acumen.

Why this emphasis on observing? It is the most fundamental skill in science and yet it is often overlooked. Kids aren't used to observing and reporting what they see. If they learn nothing else from this project, they should learn how to observe and report.

Here are a few questions to ask:

What did the car do?
Why did the car turn?
Why did it jump at the end of the ramp?
Why didn't the car go farther?
How can you get the car to travel farther?

After observation, the second most important skill students will build in this project is the ability to look for the causes of observed effects. Kids will give the strangest answers when you ask why a car did something. Get them to look at the car and the ramp and come up with a plausible answer for your "why" question. When they have a plausible answer, ask them how to confirm if the answer is right. They could run a scientific experiment to verify their answer!

## Testing

Cars should roll easily across a smooth floor or down a cardboard or wooden ramp propped up on stairs. If not, check that the wheels are free to turn (the wheels aren't rubbing on the chassis and the axles aren't rubbing on the bearings) and that the axles are parallel.

Building a small fleet of these cars provides opportunities to race them, either for speed down a ramp or for distance from the base of the ramp to the far reaches of the classroom or gym. Add weights (fishing weights, metal washers, etc.) to see if the cars perform better. Measure and record each trial run.

Record the best distance each team achieves by writing the team name and distance on the board. This simple act will provide additional incentive for teams to keep working to improve their models.

## Variations

Make cars of different widths and lengths, and use different materials for the chassis. Try different wheel sizes and placements.

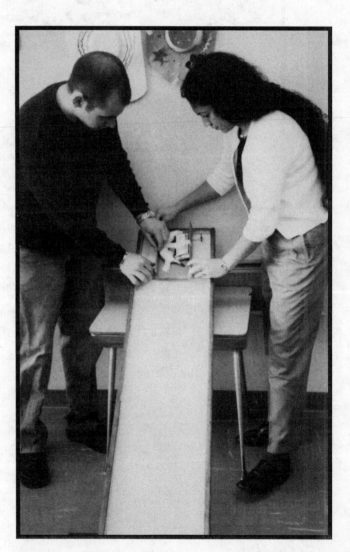

Teachers in a *Loco-Motion* workshop test their gravity car on a wooden ramp.

Gravity cars can be made from a variety of inexpensive materials. Wooden wheels use ¼-inch axles and fat straws for bearings. Plastic wheels use ⅛-inch dowels and regular straws.

Then get creative with the number of wheels. Making a car with four wheels is simple. Try making one with three wheels.

The next several projects use the gravity-powered car as a platform for different power sources.

Name: _____

# Gravity-Powered Car

## CHALLENGE

Design, build, and demonstrate a model car that is powered by gravity. It should roll down a ramp and across the floor as far as possible. Keep improving your car to make it go farther.

## DESIGN

Sketch a picture of your car below, showing the number and placement of wheels and axles and the size and shape of the car body.

Name: _____

# Gravity-Powered Car

## INSTRUCTIONS FOR INVENTORS

1. With approval from the design chief (your teacher), use cardboard and scissors to cut out the car body. Use the materials your teacher provides to make wheels, axles, and bearings.

2. Add bearings. To align the bearings (straws), draw 2 straight lines parallel to each other on the bottom of the car body. If the bearings and axles aren't parallel, the car won't travel far.

3. Cut two bearings from a straw. They should be about as wide as the car body. Glue or tape them onto the car along the lines you drew.

4. Add axles. Cut axles or ask your design chief to cut them. Axles need to be longer than the bearings. Slide the axles into the bearings and check to see if they turn easily.

5. Add wheels. Fit wheels onto the axles. You can tap them on with your hand.

6. Test your car. Roll it on the floor. Does it travel in a straight line? If not, find the problem and correct it. Does it roll easily, or does it stop as soon as you stop pushing it? If it stops soon, find the problem and fix it.

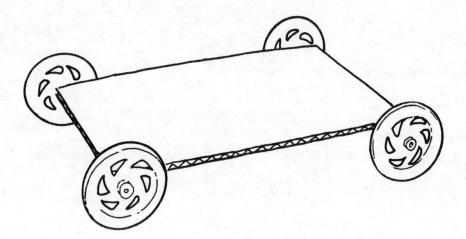

Gravity cars can be made from a variety of inexpensive materials. Wooden wheels use ¼-inch axles and fat straws for bearings. Plastic wheels use ⅛-inch dowels and regular straws.

Name: _____

# Gravity-Powered Car

## TEST

Release your car from the top of the ramp and watch what it does. If your car travels more than a few feet beyond the end of the ramp, measure the distance it covers and record it below. If not, figure out what is preventing the car from going farther and fix it.

   Record the distance your car travels. Then make improvements to your car so it will travel farther. Record what you did and how far the car went.

| Experiment number | What was changed? | Distance (include units) |
| --- | --- | --- |
| 1 | Initial design (no change) | |
| 2 | | |
| 3 | | |
| 4 | | |
| 5 | | |
| 6 | | |
| 7 | | |

Name: _____

# Gravity-Powered Car

In the preceding experiments you released your car from the top of the ramp to give it maximum energy. Now try releasing the car from lower heights and measuring how far your car will travel. As you use lower starting locations—and, therefore, lower energies—what do you think will happen to the resulting distance the car travels?

Run the experiments at 10 different heights, measured vertically from the floor to the place on the ramp where you release the car. Be consistent in how you take the measurements. For example, you might measure from the floor to the ramp and place the front wheels at that point. Whatever method you choose for the first measurement, repeat this action for each subsequent measurement.

| Height above the floor (units) | Distance the car travels (units) |
|---|---|
|  |  |
|  |  |
|  |  |
|  |  |
|  |  |
|  |  |
|  |  |
|  |  |

Name: _____

# Gravity-Powered Car

## REFLECT

What was the source of energy that propelled your car?

_____

_____

_____

_____

_____

What was the effect of friction on your car's progress?

_____

_____

_____

_____

_____

What could you do to make the car go farther?

_____

_____

_____

_____

_____

# Balloon Racer

## Challenge

Design, build, and test a car powered by an inflated balloon. Get the car to travel as far as possible in a straight line.

## Overview

This very engaging problem will captivate students in elementary school through graduate school. It's easy to "know" how the balloon racer works, but it's more difficult to make one work well.

## Materials

Cardboard (1 large box or 2 small boxes)
Fat straws (2 per team)
¼″ dowels and wooden wheels or ⅛″ dowels and plastic wheels
Latex balloons, 10″ × 12″ diameter (2 per team)
Hot glue
Tape
Vinyl tubing
Masking tape, 1″ wide
Scissors
Measuring sticks or tape
Wire cutters (for cutting dowels)

Although you can make balloon racers without the vinyl tubing, the tubing makes construction and operation easier. It also allows students to run additional experiments to evaluate the optimal size of tubing (both diameter and length) for maximum car propulsion. Purchase tubing at hardware stores for a few cents per foot. Consider using two to three feet of several diameters, from ¼-inch inside diameter (ID) to ¾-inch ID. Students can cut lengths of their choosing from the tube they select.

## Design Concept

This activity adds a propulsive force to the basic (gravity) car in the previous activity. Insert a short section of a tube into the mouth of a balloon and tape it in place to prevent air from escaping around the tube. Use a generous dollop of hot glue on the cardboard chassis to secure the vinyl tube.

## Getting Started

If possible, reserve a gym or other large room with smooth floor. Create a start line by laying down a five-foot length of masking tape on the floor. From the start line,

Vinyl tubing vents air from the balloon and provides a convenient place to attach the balloon racer motor to the chassis.

mark off every five-foot (or two-meter) interval and label the distance by writing on strips of masking tape. If you want students to measure distances precisely, provide meter sticks so they can measure from the intervals you label.

To cut the dowels, use a sharp wire cutter to notch the dowels all the way around. Snap the dowel at the notch to break it. Or, use a coping saw to make a clear cut. Students in grades four and above can use coping saws safely and most would benefit from the experience of cutting wood with a saw, so consider letting them cut their own axles. Vices or clamps make this job easier.

Label the diameters of the pieces of tubing and have students record the sizes of their pieces. On the board, record the maximum distances achieved, updating the board every time a new record is set.

## Teachable Moments

The first challenge is for students to get their cars to roll easily and travel in a straight line. Instruct students to push their models by hand to see how easily they move. If the cars stop quickly, ask students why their cars aren't going very far. Some will recognize that the wheels are rubbing against the straws or car bodies, and will know what to do. For students who do not recognize the problem, suggest they turn the cars over and spin the wheels by hand. If they still don't see the problem, ask if the wheels or axles are rubbing on anything. Mention that friction drains energy and limits how far a car will travel.

If the cars turn to one side rather than travel in a straight line, first ask the students what their cars did. When they can report that the car turned (they may need to repeat the experiment to recognize this), ask them why it turned. Many will toss out ideas without looking at the car. Suggest they look at the underside of the car. If they don't recognize the problem, ask them how cars turn corners (the front axle pivots in the direction of the turn). Ask them to look at the front axle to see if it is parallel to the rear axle.

A few students may set their cars on the start line backward. Let them run the experiment to recognize the error. If they don't understand what happened, ask them to stand up and pretend they're about to roller skate: "To move forward, what direction do you push with your feet?" Skaters and a balloon have to push backward to accelerate forward.

## Testing

Test balloon racers on the floor. Mark the starting place with a piece of masking tape. Consider marking distances along a straight track every five feet, (or one and a half meters) from the start. Students can then measure from these marks instead of having to measure from the start line each time. The only distance that counts is the straight-line distance from the starting line—in a direction perpendicular to the starting line.

## Variations

If a short piece of tubing helps direct the flow of air, will a long piece help more? To answer this question, students may cut a piece of tubing several inches long. Air moving through the tube will slow down due to friction with the tube walls, delivering less forward motion to the car. Suggest they cut the tube shorter and measure the distance the car travels.

Some will want to try using two balloons, thinking that twice the power will deliver twice the distance. Require that they complete a one-balloon car and then allow them to try two. Rarely does adding a second balloon improve distance. It's too difficult to get the two balloons to both blow in the right direction (directly behind the car) and avoid interfering with each other or getting tangled up under the wheels.

One two-balloon design does work but is difficult to inflate: insert one balloon inside another. The added elastic pressure from the second balloon can add significant distance.

Record on the board the distances achieved with different size tubing. Students should see that improvement doesn't always occur by making something bigger or smaller. In engineering and inventing the trick is often to find the optimal size or design.

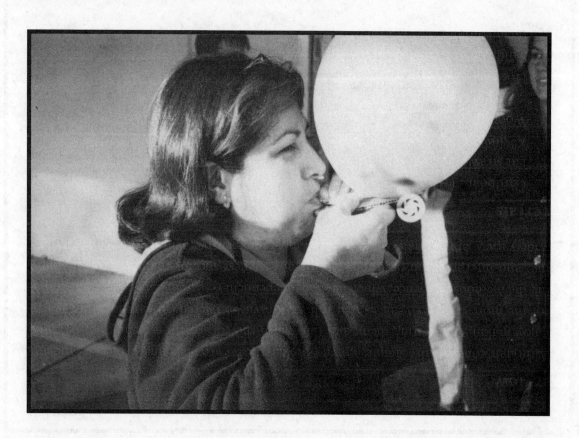

Name: _____

# Balloon Racer

## CHALLENGE

Design, build, and demonstrate a model car that is powered by a balloon. Improve the design to maximize the distance your car travels.

## DESIGN

Start by sketching a picture below of your car showing the number and placement of wheels, size and shape of the car body, location of the balloon engine, and direction of travel.

# Balloon Racer

## INSTRUCTIONS FOR INVENTORS

1. With approval from the design chief (your teacher), use scissors to cut out the car body from a piece of cardboard.

2. Add bearings. To align the bearings, draw 2 straight lines parallel to each other on the bottom of the car body. If the bearings and axles aren't parallel, the car won't travel very far.

3. Cut 2 bearings from a straw. They should be about as wide as the car body. Glue or tape them onto the car along the lines you drew.

4. Add axles. Cut axles or ask your design chief to cut them. They need to be longer than the bearings. Slide the axles into the bearings and check to see if they turn easily.

5. Add wheels. Fit the wheels onto the axles by tapping them on with your hand.

6. Test your car. Roll it on the floor. Does it go straight? If not, fix the problem before adding the balloon engine. Does it roll easily, or does it stop as soon as you stop pushing it? If the car stops when you stop pushing it, find the problem and fix it.

7. Add the engine. Select a size of vinyl tubing and cut a short piece to use. Record the size of the tubing here:

   Tube diameter: _____ (units) _____

   Tube length: _____ (units) _____

8. Insert the tube into the mouth of a balloon. If the tube is narrow enough to slide out of the balloon, hold the balloon in place with a piece of tape or a rubber band. Use hot glue to attach the tube to the car body.

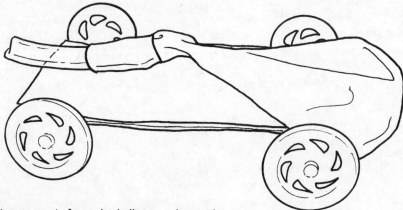

Vinyl tubing vents air from the balloon and provides a convenient place to attach the balloon racer motor to the chassis.

Name: _____

# Balloon Racer

## TEST

At the start line, inflate the balloon fully. Pinch the balloon above the tube or hold a finger over the end of the tube to keep the balloon inflated until you're ready to release it. Place the car on the start line and release your grip. Measure how far the car goes.

Record the distance your car travels. Then make improvements to your car so it will travel farther. Note the changes you made, test the car at the start line, and record how far the car travels.

| Experiment number | What was changed? | Distance (include units) |
|---|---|---|
| 1 | Initial design (no change) | |
| 2 | | |
| 3 | | |
| 4 | | |
| 5 | | |
| 6 | | |
| 7 | | |

Name: _____

# Balloon Racer

What role do you think the nozzle (vinyl tubing) plays? Compare your best results to those of other teams that used different size tubes. Record them here, including your own results.

| Tube size (diameter) | Maximum distance (units) |
| --- | --- |
|  |  |
|  |  |
|  |  |
|  |  |
|  |  |

## REFLECT

Do larger or smaller nozzles provide the farthest travel distance?

_____

_____

_____

_____

_____

_____

Name: _____

# Balloon Racer

Does your car travel at the same speed throughout its runs or does it accelerate (gain speed) and decelerate (lose speed)? Perform another experiment and watch the speed of the car so you can report when it travels slowly, fast, and faster.

| | |
|---|---|
| While you're holding the car | It isn't moving. |
| Just after releasing the car | The car is moving _____. |
| In the middle of the run | The car is moving _____. |
| Near the end of the run | The car is moving _____. |
| At the end | The car has stopped. |

Why does the car change speed throughout the run? Give specific answers for each of the 5 time periods in the chart above.

1. _____

2. _____

3. _____

4. _____

5. _____

## EXTEND

How could you use a second balloon to make the car go farther? If time permits, get the materials you need and give it a try. Record how this car performs compared to your first car.

Name: _____

# Balloon Racer

The 2-balloon car traveled _____ (units) _____, compared to

the 1-balloon car, which traveled _____ (units) _____. Why do
you think the car performed differently?

_____

_____

_____

_____

_____

_____

_____

# Electric Car: Propeller-Drive

There are several ways to use the energy stored in batteries to power a model car. Kids can learn the elements of direct current (dc) circuits by making cars that utilize battery power differently. Propeller cars are the easiest electric cars to build.

## Challenge

Design and build a battery-powered car that uses a propeller. Get the car to travel as fast as possible in a straight line.

## Overview

Inexpensive electric motors spin at high speeds, typically 12,000–17,000 revolutions per minute (rpm). These speeds are too high for direct drive applications, but are perfect for propellers.

This activity offers students opportunities to learn about forces, energy, motion, velocity, and simple direct current circuits, without requiring long introductions, lectures, or reading.

You will find that students will want to keep building and testing these cars. Capitalize on their enthusiasm by allowing them time to experiment, while still requiring them to record observations and collect and analyze data.

## Materials

Cardboard (1 large box or 2 small boxes)
Scissors (1 pair per team)
9 V batteries (1 per team, plus spares)
Electric motors (1 per team)
Propellers (1 per team)
Alligator clip leads (at least 2 per team)
Wooden wheels (4 per team) and ¼″ dowels (budget 8″× 10″ per team)
 or plastic wheels and ⅛″ dowels
Fat straws
Hot glue
Tape
Stopwatches or a clock with a second hand

Purchase the propellers and motors from the same vendor or take steps to ensure that the propellers will fit on to the motor shafts. Provide extra motors and batteries for teams to use in advanced projects.

Either allow students to cut dowels with a coping saw or have them request that you cut dowels with a wire cutter. You should cut the dowels for students in grades lower than third grade. Above third grade, kids can cut the dowel with a coping saw. Placing the dowel in a vice makes the task easier and safer.

## Design Concept

Students will encounter a number of learning challenges. Some of the common ones are listed here. However, I suggest that you do not offer the solutions to these problems to the students. Instead, encourage teams to solve them and share information with each other.

In most cases in which a car won't move forward, the wheels aren't large enough to give the propeller clearance above the ground unless a motor mount (such as a folded piece of cardboard) is inserted underneath the motor. Students will discover this when they connect the battery to the motor, which will cause the propeller to hit the ground as it tries to spin.

Cars that don't roll easily on the floor with a gentle push won't travel very fast with an electric motor. If teams are having problems, suggest that they think of the car as made of two systems: the car body and wheels, and the propulsion system. If the propulsion system is working, they need to check the other system by isolating the car body and wheels system and testing only it.

## Getting Started

Pass out the motors and batteries, and have kids experiment to see how to make the motors spin. One motor terminal must touch one battery terminal, and the other motor terminal

Testing propeller cars energizes the participants in a workshop.

must touch the other battery terminal for the motor to turn. That is, the electrical circuit must be complete. Reversing the polarity (switching the battery so the positive [+] terminal contacts the motor contact previously connected to the negative [–] terminal) reverses the direction of spin.

## Teachable Moments

If students haven't observed dc circuits before, they may become befuddled when they connect the battery to the motor and the car moves in the wrong direction. This is a great opportunity to interrupt a team and pose the question: "How many different ways can you solve this problem?" Don't let them continue until they have considered at least two ways and decided which one will work best.

If a car travels in an unintended direction, teams can correct the problem by reversing the leads from the battery to the motor or reversing the position of the motor itself.

## Testing

Prepare a racecourse with a start and end line. Measure the distance between the two lines and write that number on the board. As teams record the time it takes for their cars to complete runs, have them calculate the speed. Speed is distance divided by time. So, if a car covered a 5 meter racecourse in 2 seconds, the speed would be 2.5 meters per second.

## Variations

Students can try a variety of propellers to see which design works best. Propellers typically come in two-blade, three-blade, or four-blade models. Older students can make their own propellers out of aluminum foil or form them out of a light wood using sanding blocks or wood-shaping tools. Making propellers out of aluminum foil allows students to vary the pitch of the blade easily.

A wide-body car could support two motors and two propellers side by side. Or students could mount a pulling motor and a pushing motor on a narrow car. Does a model with two motors travel faster than a model with one motor (both using a single battery for power)? Does a two-motor and two-battery model go twice as fast? Suggest that they test the models.

Teams that finish early can extend the activity by making their models remote controled. Provide each team with a potentiometer (0×100 ohm linear taper, available from electronics stores and catalogs) and a number of 22-gauge wire pieces and wire strippers. Potentiometers are variable resistors. By placing one in series in the circuit, students change the resistance of the circuit and hence the current.[1] The voltage provided by the battery (nine volts) pushes current at a rate determined by the total resistance in the circuit, as expressed by the formula V=IR, where V is voltage (volts), I is current (amperes), and R is resistance (ohms). With the potentiometer rotated to its zero-ohm position (rotated counterclockwise), the motor turns at the same speed as it did before the potentiometer was introduced. As students rotate the potentiometer to raise resistance, the circuit current is reduced and the propeller slows. At full resistance, the motor stops turning.

Using long wires to connect the potentiometer to the onboard circuit allows students to walk beside their car while they control its speed. Thus, they can control the car remotely.

A multimeter (which costs about fifteen dollars) allows students to measure the resistance of the potentiometer and observe what it does in an electrical circuit. They could measure the voltage of the battery and the voltage drop across the motor and across the potentiometer. Added together, the voltage drops across the motor and potentiometer will equal the voltage supplied by the battery. If the multimeter measures current too, they can put the meter in series in the circuit and measure the current. Current multiplied by the resistance of the circuit will equal the voltage.

---

[1]To connect a potentiometer, disconnect one of the alligator clip leads from one of the battery terminals, and attach the clip to one of the end terminals of the potentiometer. Connect a third alligator clip lead to the other end terminal of the potentiometer and the open battery terminal.

Name: _____

# Electric Car: Propeller-Drive

## CHALLENGE

Design, build, and test a car powered by an electric motor with propeller.

## DESIGN

Sketch a design for your team's car showing the placement of the motor and propeller and the number and placement of wheels. Draw how you will connect the battery to the motor. When your team agrees on the design, show it to your design chief (teacher) before collecting materials to make the car.

Name: _____

# Electric Car: Propeller-Drive

## INSTRUCTIONS FOR INVENTORS

There are two systems to build, so consider having different team members tackle the systems—with everyone following the team design.

### System 1: Car Body and Wheels

1. Cut the car body out of cardboard. Use hot glue to secure straws to the bottom of the body to act as bearings for the axles (dowels). Make sure that the bearings are parallel to each other.

2. Cut the dowels into lengths long enough that they'll slide through the bearings and extend beyond the length of the bearings (straws), and attach wheels. If the wheels slide around the axles, put a tiny dab of hot glue into the hole of the wheel so it touches both wheel and axle.

3. When the glue has dried, test the car body by gently pushing it along the floor. Does it travel in a straight line? Does it continue to travel after you release it? If not, fix the problems before adding the motor.

### System 2: Propulsion

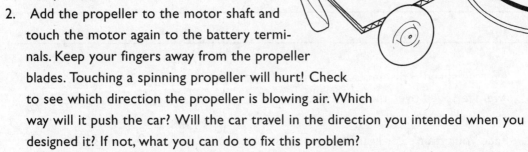

1. Test the motor by touching the motor terminals to the terminals of the 9 V battery. The motor should spin at a high speed and emit a whiny sound.

2. Add the propeller to the motor shaft and touch the motor again to the battery terminals. Keep your fingers away from the propeller blades. Touching a spinning propeller will hurt! Check to see which direction the propeller is blowing air. Which way will it push the car? Will the car travel in the direction you intended when you designed it? If not, what you can do to fix this problem?

3. Connect the propulsion system to the car body. First, hold the motor in position to see if it works where you intend to put it. If so, tape the motor to the body to hold it in place.

4. Use another piece of tape to secure the 9 V battery to the car body. Then connect 1 alligator clip lead from a motor terminal to a battery terminal. Coil the excess wire and tape it to the car body to keep it out of the way. When the car is ready to test, connect the second clip lead from the motor to the available battery terminal.

Name: _____

# Electric Car: Propeller-Drive

## TEST

Once the wires are connected, the propeller will spin wildly, driving the car forward (or backward, depending on how you connected the wires and attached the propeller).

Demonstrate to your design chief that your car works. Then demonstrate how to reverse the direction of the car. Show how to move the car in all the directions you can imagine.

A track measured on the floor can help you test your car. To make your own test track, mark a start line on a smooth floor with a piece of masking tape. Locate the finish line 10 feet (3 meters) away from the start.

Start the car with its front wheels on the start line. When the propeller begins twirling, start a stopwatch (or start counting seconds on a wall clock) and continue counting until the front wheels cross the finish line. Repeat this experiment twice more and calculate the average time and average speed. (Speed is the distance the car traveled divided by the time it took to cover that distance).

Distance = _____ (units) _____

| Trial # | Time (seconds) |
|---------|----------------|
| 1 | |
| 2 | |
| 3 | |
| Average | |

Average speed = distance divided by average time
Average speed over the short course:_____ (units) _____

Race your team's car against other cars. Or try a hill climb; see how steep a ramp your car can climb. Make the ramp out of a large sheet of cardboard or wood, with one end supported by a book or brick.

Name: _____

# Electric Car: Propeller-Drive

## REFLECT

Energy is stored in the batteries as chemical energy. The chemicals react to transform the energy into electricity. The electricity flows through the wires to the motor where it is converted into kinetic (motion) energy. Where does the energy go from here?

Touch the motor to get a clue. _____

    To make the car go faster without changing the battery or motor, what could you change? Be specific in what changes you would make.

_____

    Would adding a second motor help if you didn't add a second battery?

_____

Why or why not?

_____

# Electric Car: Propeller-Drive

## EXTEND

If you enjoyed making and testing the propeller cars, consider running another science project using propeller cars. Operate a car powered by different voltages (created through a battery or combination of batteries) and calculate how fast the car travels at each voltage. Measure the time it takes to cover a known distance (say 10 feet) for each voltage. Graph the distances on one axis with the applied voltage on the other axis. The resulting graph will illustrate how voltage affects motor speed, as measured by car speed.

Use AA or C batteries to supply different voltages. Each battery provides 1.5 V dc (direct current). So, hooking up two batteries gives 3 V. Use tape or rubber bands to hold wires or clip leads to the battery terminals. Make sure you connect the positive terminal of batteries to the negative terminals of adjacent batteries. The positive terminal at the end of the battery pack connects to one terminal of the motor. The negative terminal at the other end of the battery pack connects to the other motor terminal.

Repeat measurements for voltage using several different voltages to obtain enough data to make a graph that conveys how changing voltage changes the speed of the car. Two data points would suggest a straight-line relationship, but that might not be the case. For example, the increase in speed could be related to the square root of the increase in voltage, and this would show as a curved line. Three data points could confirm a straight-line relationship or suggest a more complex relationship. The more data points you include, the more likely the graph will represent the relationship accurately.

# Electric Car: Direct-Drive

## Challenge

Design, build, and test cars powered directly by one or two electric motors.

## Overview

Direct-drive cars are conceptually the simplest motorized cars to design but are more difficult to engineer than propeller cars. The choice of materials determines the difficulty.

## Materials

Cardboard (1 large box or 2 small boxes)

Scissors (1 pair per team)

9 V batteries (check the motor specifications—
  1 battery per team, plus spares)

Gearhead motors (1 per team)

Alligator clip leads (at least 2 per team, plus spares)

Wheels (4 per team)

¼" dowels (8"×10" per team)

Fat straws (2 per team)

Hot glue

Cable ties (4 per team)

Tape

Stopwatch (1 per team) or clock with a minute hand

Bushings (optional) or hand drill and bits

Wire and wire strippers

Potentiometers, 0×100 ohms and linear taper (optional)

Gearhead motors, plastic wheels, and bushings can be purchased from Kelvin and other suppliers. Wooden wheels and dowels are sold by Woodworks.

The inexpensive direct current motors used in the other activities don't work well here; they spin too fast. One alternative is to make a reduction gear—and that conceptual approach is taken in the following activity. Here, I recommend using gearhead motors. These dc motors come with attached gearing that greatly reduce the rate of spin (measured in rpm or revolutions per minute). These motors cost about ten to fifteen dollars.

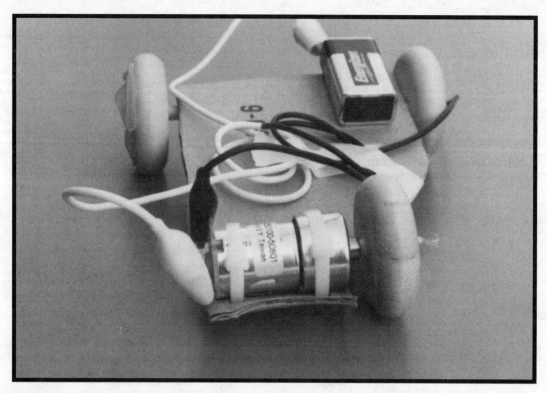

The direct-drive car uses a gearhead motor to provide slower shaft speeds.

The second problem students will encounter is how to attach the wheels to the motors. Typically, motor shafts are two millimeters long. The length of the wheel center openings in the wooden wheels I recommend for most projects is ¼ inch (6.4 mm), much larger than the motor shafts. Older students given time to calculate can solve this problem. To reduce the difficulty of the activity, purchase plastic wheels with center holes that match the diameter of the motor shafts. Or provide bushings (components that accommodate the two different sizes); these are usually made of plastic or rubber. You can make bushings by drilling a two-millimeter hole in the end of a dowel and cutting the bushing so the undrilled end goes into a wheel and the other end connects to the motor. A third option is to wrap the motor shaft in layers of masking tape, force the shaft into the wheel hole, and secure it with a drop of hot glue.

## Design Concept

Each drive wheel is connected directly to a gearhead motor. To enable steering use two gearhead motors per car. Cable ties hold the motors snugly in place without hot glue.

## Getting Started

Distribute the gearhead motors and batteries to the class. Ask students what is different about these motors from the other motors used to make other models. They will

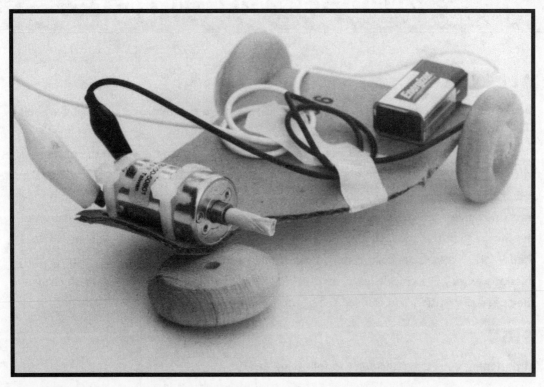

The gearhead motor shaft is wrapped in masking tape as a bushing so it fits snugly into the wheel.

recognize that these motors are larger, heavier, and spin much slower. Ask them to think what might be inside that makes them larger, heavier, and spin slower. The answer is gears. These motors have a gear system attached to a standard dc motor to reduce the rotation speed of the output shaft.

## Testing

Lay out two measured courses on a smooth floor that students can use to test their cars. One should be five feet (or two meters) long. The second should be ten feet (or three meters) long. Mark the start and finish lines with masking tape.

## Variations

Teams can make remote controls (or wire controls) by inserting long pieces of wire in the circuit that delivers power to the motors. Adding potentiometers (variable resistors) to the circuits allows students to control the speed of their motors. The long wires allow them to control the speed while standing or walking beside the model. Adding a double pole–double throw switch (available at electronics stores) makes reversing motor directions easier for advanced projects.

Name: _____

# Electric Car: Direct-Drive

## CHALLENGE

Design and build a direct-drive electric car. Direct drive means that the driving wheels are connected directly to the motors.

Cars and trucks on the road use systems of gears to change the speed of rotation from the high speeds that the engine or motor outputs to the low speeds the wheels require. Drivers control the gears through a manual transmission, or an automatic transmission changes the gears without human intervention based on the speed of rotation of the motor. (See the book *The Way Things Work* by David Macaulay or the Web site How Stuff Works [http://science.howstuffworks.com/gear.htm] for an explanation of how transmissions work.) Even model cars, such as r/c (radio controlled) cars use gears to change the speed of rotation. You can see the gears if you take an r/c car apart.

## DESIGN

In designing your car, consider the following questions:

How many motors will you use?
How many wheels do you want your car to have?
Which of the wheels will be drive wheels?
Will you be able to steer the car?
Should the car be light or heavy?

Sketch your design in the space below, illustrating your answers to the questions above.

# Electric Car: Direct-Drive

## INSTRUCTIONS FOR INVENTORS

1. You can change your design as you learn more during the building and testing phases. When your teacher has approved your design, collect materials and start building.

2. Cut the car frame out of cardboard. Attach nondrive wheels by gluing or taping a piece of a straw to the bottom of the frame. Cut a dowel (which will serve as axle) a bit longer than the width of the car. Insert the dowel through the straw (which will serve as a bearing). Attach wheels to the axle.

3. Check to see if the motor shaft will fit snugly into the hole in a wheel. If the shaft is too small, either make a bushing or ask your teacher to supply you with a bushing to connect the shaft and the wheel. Drill a hole the size of the motor shaft into one end of a short section of dowel. Insert the motor shaft into the hole. Push the other end of the dowel into a wheel.

4. Tape the motors to the frame as your sketched design shows. Tape the 9 V battery to the top of the frame. Use clip leads to connect the battery to the motor, but don't make the last connection until you are ready to test the car.

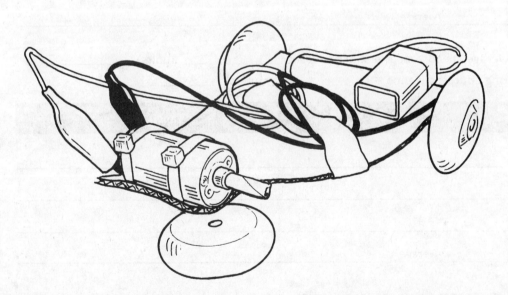

The gearhead motor shaft is wrapped in masking tape as a bushing so it fits snugly into the wheel.

Name: _____

# Electric Car: Direct-Drive

## TEST

Place the car on the floor and complete the circuit. Does the car move? If not, observe if the motor spins when you pick up the car. There could be problems with the wiring, connections, battery, or motors.

If the motor spins when the wheels aren't touching the floor, the battery might be too weak. Try replacing the battery or using a battery with a higher voltage. Also examine the car to ensure that the drive wheels aren't rubbing on anything.

When the car is functional and can travel in a straight line, measure its speed. Run 3 tests on both the shorter and longer measured courses. Record the times and the course distances here.

Short course: distance = _____ (units) _____

| Trial # | Time (seconds) |
|---------|----------------|
| 1       |                |
| 2       |                |
| 3       |                |
| Average |                |

Average speed over the short course: _____ (units) _____

Long course: distance = _____ (units) _____

| Trial # | Time (seconds) |
|---------|----------------|
| 1       |                |
| 2       |                |
| 3       |                |
| Average |                |

Average speed over the long course: _____ (units) _____

How do the 2 average speeds compare? Why are there differences between the 2?

_____

_____

# Electric Car: Direct-Drive

## EXTEND

If you used 1 motor on your first model, try making a car with 2 motors. Use 1 battery to drive the 2 motors. Do you expect the 2-motor car will go faster or slower than the first model? _____

Test your answer by repeating the experiment above for the 2-motor cars. Record your data and results here:

Short course: distance = _____ (units) _____

| Trial # | Time (seconds) |
|---------|----------------|
| 1 | |
| 2 | |
| 3 | |
| Average | |

Average speed over the short course: _____ (units) _____

Which model car was faster? Why?

## Additional Projects

1. Try to design and build a direct-drive car that will go faster than either of the other 2 cars. Ask your teacher to approve your design and then build and test your ideas.

2. Can you make your car turn in a circle? How many different ways can you do this?

3. Create a remote control device that allows you to start and stop your car while standing at least 3 feet away.

4. Create a remote control device that allows you to move the car forward and in reverse while you are standing at least 3 feet away.

5. Use a potentiometer (variable resistor) to change the speed of the car through remote control.

# Electric Car: Belt-Drive

## Challenge

Design, build, and race model cars powered by electric motors, using rubber bands to transfer the power to drive wheels.

## Overview

One way to transfer power from the motor to the wheels is through a belt. Entire factories were once powered by belts turned by water, wind, or steam power. In this activity, rubber bands not only transfer the power from motor to wheel, they also provide gearing and traction for the wheel.

## Materials

Cardboard (1 large box or 2 small boxes)

Wooden wheels, 2″ diameter, ¼″ center hole (4 per team)

¼″ dowels (at least 16″ per team)

Fat straws (2 per team)

Hot glue

Rubber bands (6 per team)

Aluminum soda cans (1 per team)

Direct current electric motors (1 per team, plus spares)

9 V battery (1 per team, plus spares)

Alligator clip leads (2 per team, plus spares)

Awl

Pliers

Scissors (1 per team)

Stopwatches (1 per team) or a clock with a second hand

Craft sticks (6 per team)

## Design Concept

Creative students may come up with several ways to make a motorized belt-drive car. The design I suggest uses a soda can as the drive wheel. A rubber band conveys power from the motor shaft to the can. The can is supported on an axle made from a dowel. To hold the can in place, the axle passes through a wheel that is glued to each end of the can. Students may have to reinforce the car frame to keep it from bending and may have to use craft sticks or a dowel to help hold the motor in place against the tension of the rubber band.

## The Details

Students often have a difficult time visualizing how to make this model. If time is limited, show them a model that you've made. The downside of showing your model is that most teams will mimic it and will not exercise their creative design capabilities.

To help students without showing them a model, point out three design features of successful cars:

1. The wheels fit onto the dowels and the dowels fit through the fat straws to make a system that turns easily.
2. The motor spins too fast to be effective in driving the model. Stretching a rubber band from the motor shaft to a soda can greatly reduces the speed of rotation of the wheel.

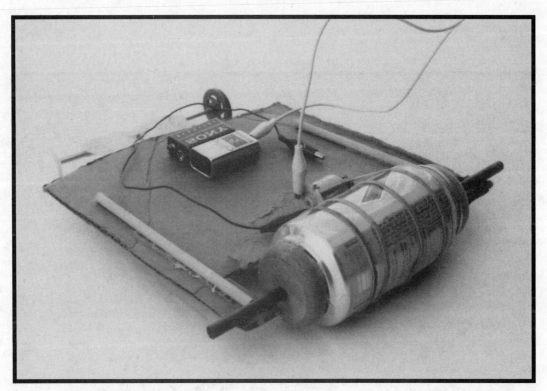

A belt drive turns the soda can wheel.

3. Placing several rubber bands around the can improves its traction and provides spare belts if one should break.

Students may exhibit frustration at not understanding how to build the model. Allow students to struggle because they will eventually rise to the activity's challenges and feel rewarded when they complete the project.

Students may also encounter difficulties with aligning the motor so the drive belt doesn't slip off. The motor needs to be aligned so its driveshaft is angled slightly away from the soda can. If the tension of the rubber band pulls the motor toward the can, a short section of dowel (or craft stick) can be secured with hot glue in front of the motor to hold it in place. Large cardboard models will require reinforcement to prevent the cardboard from buckling.

Creative students will design cars with one wheel (the drive wheel) or two wheels (motorcycle?) instead of the more obvious three-wheel car.

Two-inch wheels can be glued to the top and bottom of a soda can to hold an axle in place. Affixing the wheels this way requires poking a hole in the bottom of the can with an awl and widening the drinking hole with pliers. Be cautious of sharp metal edges.

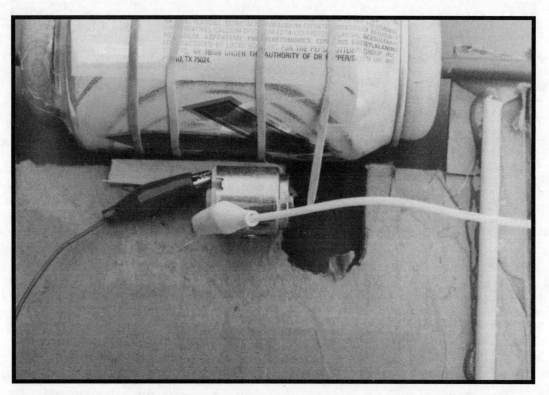

A craft stick helps hold the motor in place. One rubber band acts as a drive belt, the others provide traction for the wheels (cans).

## Getting Started

Create a test track by laying two pieces of masking tape on a smooth floor, one being the start line and one the finish line. Lay them parallel to each other, ten feet (or three meters) apart. Instruct students to test their cars on this test track. They can measure time to calculate speed.

## Teachable Moments

Students will engage in the iterative process of design, build, test, and rebuild to complete this project. They will solve several problems and operate as a design team. Help them understand their problems by framing questions. For example, if the car frame is buckling or bending, ask how they could reinforce the cardboard. Answering critical questions helps students change their focus from failure to possible solutions.

Name: _____

# Electric Car: Belt-Drive

## CHALLENGE

Build and test a car powered by a battery using a belt drive. Use an empty soda can for the drive wheel and rubber bands as belts.

## DESIGN

Look at the materials provided and think about possible designs. As you consider the possibilities, think about these questions:

How will you connect the motor to the battery?

How will you transfer the motion provided by the motor to the drive wheel?

How close should the motor be to the drive wheel, based on the elasticity of the belts?

Will the drive wheel slip on the smooth floor? What can you do to prevent it from slipping?

How many wheels should your model have? Consider alternative numbers.

What shape should the car body take to support the motor, drive wheels, and other wheels?

When you have a design in mind, sketch it below. Illustrate the number and position of wheels, the location of the motor and battery, and the place you will connect the motor and the battery. Also show how you will support the drive wheel and any other wheels.

Name: _____

# Electric Car: Belt-Drive

Show your sketch to your design chief (teacher) to gain approval to start building.

One person can cut out the car frame while another hooks up the electric system to test it. If you have a third person, he or she can prepare the wheels and bearings.

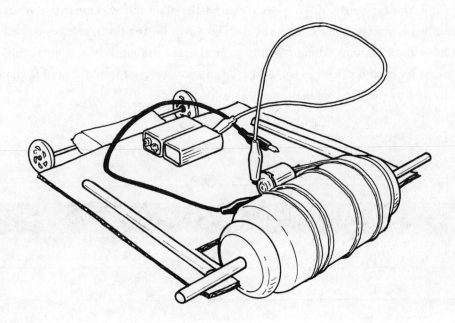

A belt drive turns the soda can wheel.

## INSTRUCTIONS FOR INVENTORS

Design questions to ask your team include the following:

How will you get spinning power from the motor to a wheel?

How will you support the drive wheel?

How will you keep the motor from moving?

How will you get sufficient traction on the drive wheel so it doesn't slip?

What size and shape do you need for the cardboard frame to accommodate the drive wheel/motor assembly?

## TEST

Demonstrate to your design chief that your car works. Then demonstrate how you can reverse the direction the car travels.

Name: _____

# Electric Car: Belt-Drive

Use the measured track that your design chief taped to the floor or create your own to test the car. To make your own track, mark a start line on a smooth floor with a piece of masking tape. Locate the finish line 10 feet (or 3 meters) away from the start.

Position the car so the drive wheel touches the start line. Connect the wires to start the drive wheel spinning, then set the car down on the floor, release the car, and start timing the run. Stop timing when the car crosses the finish line. Repeat this experiment twice and calculate the average time and average speed. Speed is the distance divided by the time it takes to cover that distance:

Speed = Distance/Time

Distance = _____ (units) _____

| Trial # | Time (seconds) |
|---------|----------------|
| 1 | |
| 2 | |
| 3 | |
| Average | |

Average speed over the short course: _____ (units) _____

Name: _____

# Electric Car: Belt-Drive

What could you do to increase the speed of your car? List some ideas here. Show them to your teacher for approval and implement 1 or more of your ideas.

Ideas to improve the car's speed:

1. _____

2. _____

3. _____

4. _____

5. _____

Describe your success in improving the car's speed. What was your fastest time and speed?

Time = _____ (seconds)

Speed = _____ (units) _____

What change was most effective in improving speed? _____

## EXTEND

With your teacher's permission, race your car against other cars. Or use an alligator clip lead to hitch your model to another model and have the cars compete in a tractor pull (tug of war). A third option is to have cars compete in a hill climb: set up a piece of cardboard as a ramp and see whose car can climb highest.

## REFLECT

Compare the speed of rotation of the motor to the speed of rotation of the drive wheel. Even though they are connected by a rubber band, why do they spin at different speeds? _____

What other machines have wheels turning faster or slower than the driving force or motor? _____

Where else do you see belts or similar devices used to connect wheels and gear systems? _____

List several ways you could make the wheels spin slower.

_____

_____

# Hovercraft

## Challenge

Design and build a model hovercraft that will slide easily across a smooth surface.

## Overview

A wide variety of materials can be used in this activity. The materials listed below can be used to make a simple version of a hovercraft.

## Materials

CDs (1 per team, use old CDs or the free promotional CDs that
  often come in the mail)
Pop-up lids from plastic water or juice bottles (1 per team)
Hot glue
Balloons (2 per team)

## Design Concept

With hot glue, secure a pop-up lid over the center hole in a CD. Inflate a balloon and stretch the mouth over the top of the pop-up lid. Close the lid to keep the air in the balloon and open the lid when ready to launch.

A discarded CD and drinking water bottle top make a hovercraft powered by an inflated balloon.

## Testing

Students can test how the size of the opening changes the characteristics of the hovercraft. Cover part of the opening in the CD with tape or glue a small rubber washer in the opening. To test how easily a hovercraft slides, use a smooth-topped table. Prop up the legs at one end of the table with books (not this one, of course) or bricks. Release the hovercraft at a variety of elevations to find out at what angle it first slides and to measure how quickly it slides off the table at different angles.

## Getting Started

The day before you do this activity, tell students that they will get to make simple hovercrafts and that they need to find out how hovercrafts (and hoverboards) work. They can check *The Way Things Work* or other library references or go to the How Stuff Works Web site at http://travel.howstuffworks.com/hoverboard.htm.

## Teachable Moments

Ask teams why a hovercraft moves easily when the balloon is exhausting through the hole and why the hovercraft doesn't move when it's not. The weight of the hovercraft is nearly the same in each case; the weight's a bit higher when the balloon is inflated. What does the escaping air do?

The escaping air lifts the hovercraft above the surface of the table, so it rides on a thin layer of air. Since the hovercraft is not in contact with the tabletop, it encounters little friction and can move easily.

## Variations

You can make a demonstration hovercraft that carries a lightweight person across a smooth floor, such as a gym floor. The "hover" is provided by a shop vac or air blower. See my book *Fantastic Flying Fun with Science* (McGraw-Hill, 2000) for construction details.

Name: _____

# Hovercraft

## CHALLENGE

Design and build a hovercraft that slides easily on a smooth surface. Find the optimal size orifice (opening) for air to pass through. That is, try different size openings to see which provides the easiest and longest slide across a table.

## INSTRUCTIONS FOR INVENTORS

1. Glue a water bottle pop-up lid to the center of a CD.

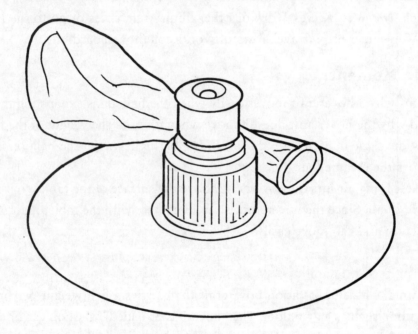

A discarded CD and drinking water bottle top make a hovercraft powered by an inflated balloon.

Name: _____

# Hovercraft

2. Attach an inflated balloon to the top of the lid. Pull up the lid when you're ready to launch.

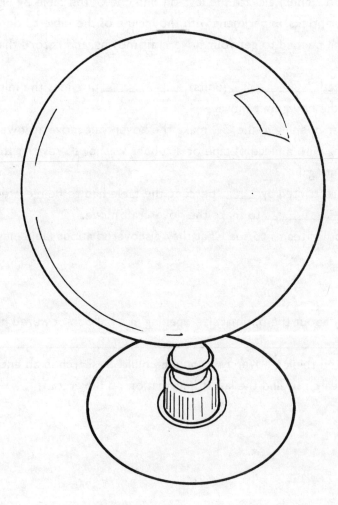

A discarded CD and drinking water bottle top make a hovercraft powered by an inflated balloon.

Name: _____

# Hovercraft

## TEST

Slide a hovercraft across a smooth surface, such as a table. With the permission of your design chief (teacher) elevate the legs on one end of the table by propping it up on some books or bricks. Experiment with the incline of the table to determine the minimum elevation needed to get your hovercraft moving, and record that information here:

A table elevated _____(units) _____ provides the minimum angle needed to make the hovercraft move.

Does a smaller opening in the CD make the hovercraft move at lower elevations? Cover the opening with a piece of tape or a rubber washer to restrict the air flow and try the experiment again.

If the hole is restricted by _____ percent, the table had to be elevated by _____(units) _____ to make the hovercraft move.

Check with other teams to see what they discovered about table elevation and air flow.

## REFLECT

What can you say about the optimal size opening in a balloon-powered hovercraft of this type? _____

How big do you think a hovercraft could be built? Research in an encyclopedia or conduct a Web search to find the latest information on hovercraft.

# Top

## Challenge

Design and build a top that spins for as long a time as possible.

## Overview

Students build tops, test them by spinning them and measuring the duration of spin, and rebuild them to spin longer. With a good launch, a top can spin for more than a minute.

## Materials

¼″ dowel

Wooden wheels with ¼″ center opening, variety of diameters

Nylon string

PVC pipe, ¾″, schedule 200 (1 8″ length will provide at least 10 launchers)

Electric drill and ⁵⁄₁₆″ bit

Scissors

Coping saw

Sand paper or sanding blocks

Stopwatches or clock with second hand

Hot glue

Pencil sharpener

Rulers

Each top made requires about eight to ten inches of dowel for a spindle and at least one wheel. Two-inch wheels make good bobs, but by providing a variety of sizes, you encourage experimentation. Students can also put several bobs on one spindle.

## Design Concept

Wooden wheels mounted on dowels (spindles) become tops. Students can spin the tops by hand or with a top launcher made from a piece of PVC pipe and a piece of string.

## The Details

Opening the bottom end of the spindle (dowel) in a pencil sharpener reduces friction and allows the top to spin longer. Larger and heavier wheels will keep a top spinning longer. However, there are limits to the size and weight that can be spun in this system.

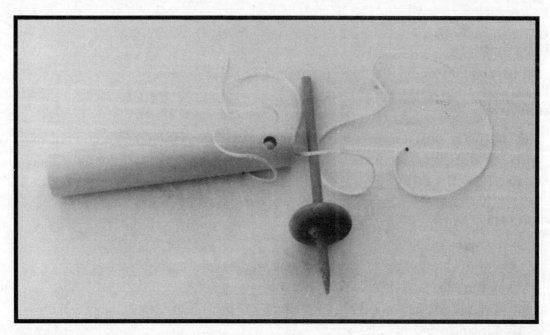

The top is made of a wooden wheel mounted on a sharpened dowel. The launcher is ¾-inch PVC pipe with a ⁵⁄₁₆-inch hole.

If the bobs (wheels) fit loosely on the spindle, suggest that students secure them with a drop of hot glue.

## Getting Started

Make several top launchers in advance. With a coping saw or other saw, cut the PVC pipe into eight-to-ten-inch lengths and sand any rough edges. Drill a ⁵⁄₁₆-inch hole through the PVC pipe about one inch from one end.

Cut strings in lengths of about twenty inches. To keep the ends of pieces of nylon string from unraveling, melt each end in the flame of a candle. Make several before the class meets. Use caution as the molten nylon can burn skin.

Note: Have teams use coping saws to cut dowels. Although some may protest about the safety

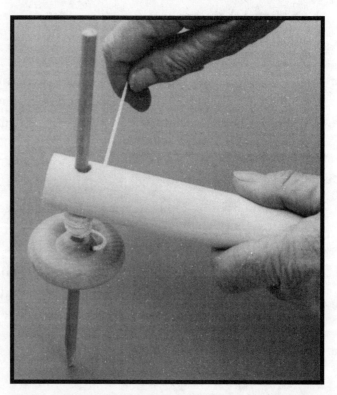

In a good launch of a top, the hand holding the launcher has to remain still, while the other hand pulls the string.

of this procedure, I find injuries rarely occur. And the experience of cutting wood provides a great opportunity for learning. Allow students to touch the side of the saw blade before and after cutting to feel the differences in temperature.

## Teachable Moments

Making and testing a top allows students to explore the science of spin and angular momentum, topics that are nearly impossible to learn through reading or lecture.

As students conduct trials, circulate among the teams to pose questions that clarify what is occurring and that ask them to consider what other experiments they can try. Ensure that the teams change one variable at a time and record the results in their logs.

A well-constructed top can spin for a minute or longer.

Ask teams why a spinning top doesn't fall over, but a nonspinning top set on its spindle does fall. Instruct teams to blow on the top while it is spinning to see what happens. (Or blow on a spinning coin). Many may expect that the top or coin will move down the airstream or fall over, but that doesn't happen.

Ask students how they stay in control when riding a bike. They are stable on the bike only when it's moving. That is, the bike is stable only when the wheels (like tops) are spinning. Ask how someone can turn a bike when riding without hands on the handlebars. This can be accomplished by leaning. However, if a person leans to one side when the bike is stationary, both the person and the bike will fall over.

Forces acting on spinning objects don't manifest themselves where the forces are applied, and that makes these forces harder to understand. The motion resulting from an applied force shows up ninety degrees down spin from where it was applied. When you lean your bike to the left, applying a force to the front wheel (the rear wheel can move side to side so you can see the effect), a nonspinning wheel will fall to the left. But, a spinning wheel will turn to the left. Instead of the top of the wheel falling to the left, the front of the wheel (ninety degrees down spin) turns to the left.

Be prepared for contradictory results. Adding weight can result in longer spins, but there is a limit to the optimal weight given the strength of the top spinner and the durability of materials. Although physics dictates that the greater the mass of the bob, the more angular momentum it will have (given that it spins at the same speed), experimentation reveals that the duration doesn't increase without limit. The angular velocity and hence momentum decrease as the mass increases, because we can't accelerate larger masses as quickly.

Make sure students understand the necessity of averaging the results from three trials. Ask for representative data from one of the teams and write the trial results on the board. Are the three durations from one experiment the same? They shouldn't be. Each time you pull the string, you pull with a slightly different force, in a slightly different direction. The results vary and we'd like to eliminate the vagaries of launching the top by averaging several trials.

Would averaging more trials be worthwhile? Look at the data. If a team's data is varied, you might suggest that the team collect more data.

Ask what useful machines could be made out of tops. To think of uses, consider the qualities of a spinning top. The spindle points constantly in the same direction and the top continues to spin for a long time. The constancy of orientation make tops good devices for stabilizing instruments. On a ship, a top (gyroscope) stabilizes a compass so it is always level even as the ship bounces around on waves. Gyrocompasses give a constant reference point from which instruments can measure angular distance. Spinning disks can provide power for motion. Take apart a "friction" toy car and you find a flywheel—not really a top, but illustrative of energy stored in rotating masses. (Friction cars are those car models that you roll forward against the floor and then release to get them to travel across the room. Rolling them against the floor gets the flywheel spinning and powers the car.) Flywheels have been used to power buses and cars.

Another use of tops is as Frisbees, tops that fly.

Name: _____

# Top

## CHALLENGE

Design, build, and test a top that spins for as long a time as possible. Test several different designs.

## DESIGN

You have several options in designing your top. How long do want the spindle (dowel) to be and what size bob (wheel) do you want to use? Where on the spindle do you want the bob to be? What should the end of the spindle look like? Sketch your design for the top below.

# Top

## INSTRUCTIONS FOR INVENTORS

1. Use a coping saw to cut the length of spindle needed for your design. Have one team member hold a dowel firmly on a table, while another team member cuts. Don't push down on the saw, just pull it back and push it forward. Let it cut all the way through the wood, and don't break the wood.

2. Slide the bob onto the spindle. If the bob slides easily around the spindle, add a drop of hot glue to hold it in place.

3. Launch the top. Wrap a piece of string around the spindle, just above the bob. Slide the top of the spindle into the holes in the top launcher. Hold the launcher horizontally (parallel to the floor), so the top's end touches the floor. Grab the end of the string with your other hand. Pull the string quickly, keeping your hand at the same level above the floor. That is, don't pull your hand upward. As soon as the top begins to spin, raise the launcher straight up and away from the spindle. Practice this several times before timing the top.

4. Troubleshoot if needed. If the spindle jams in the holes of the launcher, make sure you are keeping your pulling hand parallel to the floor. If the string slides off the spindle without spinning it, wrap the string tighter. If the top flies off to one side when you launch it, keep the hand holding the launcher still until after you are finished pulling the string.

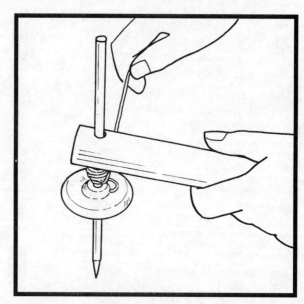

In a successful launch of a top, the hand holding the launcher (pipe) has to remain still, while the other hand pulls the string.

# Top

## TEST

One team member can record the time of each launch while another spins and releases the top. Start timing the top when it spins free of the launcher. Stop timing when the bob touches the floor.

For each test, spin the top and record the times for 3 launches. Average the 3 times and record the average in the Toy Inventor's Log below. To find the average of 3 numbers, add the 3 trials together and divide by 3.

## TOY INVENTOR'S LOG

Describe your top:

What is the size (diameter) of your bob? _____ (units) _____

How long is the spindle? _____ (units) _____

How high is the bob above the pointed end of the spindle? _____ (units) _____

| Experiment # | Modifications you made | Time Spin 1 | Time Spin 2 | Time Spin 3 | Average time |
|---|---|---|---|---|---|
| 1 | Initial design— no modifications | | | | |
| 2 | | | | | |
| 3 | | | | | |
| 4 | | | | | |
| 5 | | | | | |

Name: _____

# Top

Modify your design to produce longer spin times. Consider making any of the following changes:

a. Move the bob higher or lower on the spindle.
b. Use a longer or shorter spindle.
c. Use a larger or smaller wheel for the bob.
d. Make the end of the spindle sharper or duller (use a pencil sharpener to make it sharper).
e. Launch the top on a different surface.
f. Add a second wheel.

For each modification you try, record the result. For example, if you add weight (another wheel), did the spin time increase or decrease?

| Modifications | Impact of the modifications |
|---|---|
| | |
| | |
| | |
| | |
| | |
| | |
| | |

## REFLECT

What machines and toys make use of the properties of spin?

_____

_____

# Top

## EXTEND

With your teacher's permission, think of other ways you could test your top and launcher and perform these experiments.

Cut a circle out of a piece of lightweight, white cardboard or heavy paper. Make the circle about 5 inches in diameter. Color one half of the circle black and leave the other half white. Make a hole in the center of the paper or cardboard and slide the circle onto the spindle. Put a small dab of glue on the bob to secure the paper or cardboard to it. Now launch your top and see what colors you see. Try other combinations of colors or patterns of black and white.

A yo-yo acts like a top. Can you make a yo-yo by connecting 2 wheels on a short piece of dowel? Make a loop in the string and use the loop to tie a slipknot that you can pass over one wheel onto the dowel. Test your yo-yo to see how it works.

# Rocket Car

## Challenge

Build a car powered by air pressure that can travel as far as possible in a straight line.

## Overview

Student teams build jet cars and pressurize them with a bike pump. Building a car that travels in a straight line is a challenge in itself, and getting it to travel across a gymnasium floor will engage a wide variety of students, from fourth graders through college seniors.

If you have seen a water rocket launched that uses a two-liter soda bottle for propulsion, you know that these bottles hold high pressure. Air pressure cars don't use water as a propellant—they use air. Unlike bottle rockets, cars don't need huge liftoff forces to accelerate the bottle upward. Since the wheels support the weight of the car, the force of escaping air accelerates the car opposed only by friction and inertia.

## Materials

> Cardboard or wood veneer (2 or 3 large boxes)
> Scissors or a coping saw (1 per team)
> Hot glue
> 2-liter plastic soda bottles with lids (1 per team)
> Hand drill with bits
> Wooden wheels, 2" diameter (4 per team)
> Fat straws (2 per team)
> ¼" dowels (at least 16" per team)
> 2 or more bike pumps with gauges
> 2 inflating needles (the kind used for basketballs or footballs)
> Silly Putty (1 egg)
> Duct tape
> Safety goggles (1 pair per student)

If you don't want students to use a coping saw, have wire cutters handy so you can quickly cut the dowels to the lengths they specify. Score the dowel all the way around with the cutters and then snap off the piece.

## Design Concept

A two-liter plastic bottle makes a "battery" for storing energy that propels this car. The challenge is getting the air into the bottle and letting it exhaust slowly. If the air comes out in a second or less time, the car won't move. To get the car to travel very far, the air exhaust has to be sustained over several seconds. This requires that you make a small hole in the lid of the bottle.

## The Details

Make holes in the lids of two-liter bottles with the drill bit that's closest in size to a bike pump's inflating needle. Check to ensure that a needle will pass through the opening.

Address pressure and safety issues. To inflate the bottle, wrap a small piece of Silly Putty around the base of the inflating needle to act as a gasket. Hold the needle tightly against the lid so the putty flattens while someone else pumps the bottle. Although there is very little likelihood of the bottle exploding, wear safety goggles. At about 60 psi you won't be able to hold the needle in the bottle. This reality provides the upper limit of pressurization, which is about half of the bottle's rated pressure. If students figure out a way to inflate the bottle to higher pressures, **make sure they don't do it.**

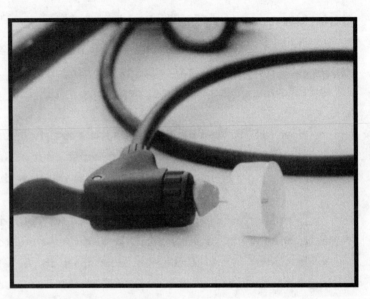

A piece of Silly Putty helps seal the air inside the rocket car until it is ready to be launched.

## Getting Started

Tape a start line on a smooth floor. Provide as much room as possible, at least seventy-five feet.

Make a model beforehand and demonstrate how it works to the class. This display will fire up their interest but won't give away any design solutions that provide learning opportunities.

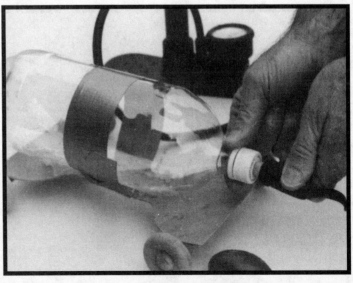

Use a bicycle pump to increase the pressure in the rocket car.

Name: _____

# Rocket Car

## CHALLENGE

Design, build, test, and improve a car powered by air pressure so it travels as far as possible. Use a bike pump to "charge" the car. Energy, in the form of air pressure, will be stored in a 2-liter bottle. Like a rocket, your car will speed across the floor.

## DESIGN

Design and build a car body with wheels that are aligned so the car travels in a straight line. Use the car-making techniques you used in prior *Loco-Motion* activities. Consider the following questions in your design:

How will you keep the car traveling in a straight line?
How can you maximize the thrust coming out of the 2-liter bottle?
How can you minimize the friction that will slow the car?

Examine the building materials provided (cardboard or wood) and decide on a size and shape for the car body. Would it be more helpful to make a large or small car? You will be adding at least 2 axles—how far apart do you want them to be? Is it better to have a narrow or wide car?

Once you have decided on the size and shape of the car, sketch the design showing the location of the wheels and the approximate length and width of the car.

Name: _____

# Rocket Car

## INSTRUCTIONS FOR INVENTORS

1.  When your design chief (teacher) has approved your design, get building materials and start to construct your car body.

2.  When you have assembled the car body and wheels, test the car by pushing it along the floor. Does it travel in a straight line? If not, correct the problem (the axles probably aren't parallel) before adding an engine.

3.  Does the car stop quickly? If so, examine the wheels or axles to see if they are rubbing on something.

4.  The engine uses a 2-liter bottle to store the energy you input when pumping the tire pump. Mount a bottle onto the car body and secure it with hot glue (lots of it) or duct tape. If the bottle isn't aligned with the car body, the escaping air will push the car to the side rather than pushing it forward.

5.  Get a lid for your bottle. If your teacher hasn't drilled a hole in the lid, carefully drill a hole using the smallest drill bit. **Be careful. Small drill bits break easily if you push them from the side. Also, make sure that you don't drill a hole into the table underneath the lid.** Turn the lid so the flat side is up. Carefully place the drill bit in the center of the lid. Then have a teammate hold the lid while you slowly turn the handle of the drill. The drill will cut through the lid in just a few seconds.

6.  Screw the lid onto the bottle.

7.  To add the pressure power required to run the car, clamp the inflating needle in the nozzle of the air pump. Around the base of the needle stretch a glob of putty so when you insert the needle into the cap the putty will form a seal.

8.  Put on safety goggles.

9.  Hold the bottle with one hand and steady the needle in the bottle with the other. Have a teammate start pumping. When the bottle reaches 40 pounds of gauge pressure, launch the car. Don't touch the car with your hand as you release it, or the car will travel off to one side.

    The bottles break above 100 psi, so you don't want to force in that much air. You'll have a hard time holding the needle in much above 50 or 60 psi, but for safety's sake don't try.

# Rocket Car

## TEST

Once you have mastered the art of launching the rocket car, conduct experiments to see how far the car travels at different pressures. Repeat each trial 3 times at each pressure and average the distances.

## TOY INVENTOR'S LOG

| Pressure | Trial 1 | Trial 2 | Trial 3 | Average Distance (units) |
|----------|---------|---------|---------|--------------------------|
| 10 psi | | | | |
| 20 psi | | | | |
| 30 psi | | | | |
| 40 psi | | | | |
| 50 psi | | | | |
| 60 psi | | | | |

What units of distance are you using? _____

Graph the results. Graph the pressure on the horizontal axis and the average distance the car traveled at that pressure on the vertical axis. Circle the data points and lightly draw a pencil line to connect them. Look at the shape of the graph. What story does the graph tell?

# Rocket Car

## REFLECT

Why does the rocket car move forward? _____

What happens if you attach the bottle at an angle to the front-rear axis of the car?

_____

## EXTEND

Pick 1 of the following experiments to try, or come up with your own. Ask for your teacher's approval before starting any advanced experiments. Do not exceed 60 psi pressure for any experiments.

1. Would the car travel farther if it had larger wheels? Change the wheel size and repeat the experiment. Graph the results on the same graph paper, labeling both lines with the wheel size each line represents.

2. Would the car travel farther if the orifice were larger? Slightly increase the diameter of the orifice. Significantly increasing the diameter will make pressurizing the bottle very difficult. Collect data as you did in the first experiment and graph the results on the same graph. Label each line to indicate which experiment used larger or smaller orifices. How does the size of the orifice affect the distance the car travels?

_____

_____

# Rubber Band Racer

## Challenge

Build and test vehicles powered by rubber bands.

## Overview

The rubber band racer is a simple vehicle that students can build and test quickly. Consider challenging them to create other designs for rubber band–powered vehicles.

## Materials

CDs for wheels (2 per team)
Toilet paper tubes or small tin cans with lids
    removed (1 per team)
Rubber bands (3–4 per team)
Metal washers (1 per team)
¼″ dowels (6″ per team)
Hot glue
Tape
Metal coat hanger
2 wire cutters or coping saws
Measuring tape or sticks (1 per team)

## Design Concept

A twisted rubber band stores energy that drives this simple mobile.

## The Details

A cardboard or metal cylinder holds the two CDs apart. A rubber band is wound up inside the cylinder to provide the driving force. Alternative designs use two wooden wheels separated by a piece of ¾-inch PVC pipe. A metal washer reduces friction between one of the CDs and the racer's dragging arm.

## Getting Started

Demonstrate a model that you've made and show how far it travels. Challenge teams to make vehicles that travel farther.

Set up a test track where teams can measure how far their racers travel. Record the results on the board by listing team names and distances.

## Teachable Moments

Ask the students what purpose the dowels play in the design. The short dowel holds one end of the rubber band in place. The longer dowel not only secures the other end of the rubber band, it also presses against the ground so the unwinding rubber band can push the racer forward. The longer dowel helps steer the racer by providing drag, similar to the rudder of a boat.

Here is a rubber band racer built from two CDs, a toilet paper tube, a rubber band, dowels, and a metal washer.

Also ask teams to trace the energy flow of the system. They input energy into the rubber band by twisting it. The rubber band stores energy and releases it by unwinding. The energy is converted into motion (kinetic energy) and eventually into heat (through friction). As teams input more energy (twist the rubber band tighter), more energy is available to drive the racer. When stretched beyond its elastic limit, a rubber band can't increase in length anymore and the material fails.

## Testing

Have teams measure and record how far their racers travel when started with different levels of energy or twists of the rubber band.

## Variations

Teams could make a rubber band–powered car using the same car body and materials as used in earlier activities.

Alternate designs for a rubber band racer use either thread spools or two wooden wheels separated by a piece of PVC pipe.

One of the problems students must overcome is getting enough traction on the driving wheels so they don't spin without moving the car. Small sections of a bike inner tube can be stretched over the wooden wheels to act as tires, improving the traction. Students can also add weight (a battery for example) over the wheels. Pickup truck drivers keep a load of sand or blocks in the truck bed in winter to provide more traction for the rear wheels.

CDs make great wheels for a rubber band racer.

Name: _____

# Rubber Band Racer

## CHALLENGE

Build and test a vehicle powered by a rubber band. Design your racer so it travels as far as possible in a straight line.

## INSTRUCTIONS FOR INVENTORS

1. Use hot glue to attach a toilet paper tube or small tin can to a CD, making sure that the tube or can is centered on the CD. Dab a bead of glue on the tube or can and hold the CD on it. Repeat the process on the other side, so the CDs form 2 wheels separated by the can or tube.

2. Slide 1 end of a rubber band through the center of 1 of the CDs. Keep it from falling through the hole by inserting a short piece of dowel through the loop. Tape or glue this dowel in place on the face of the CD.

3. Use a piece of coat hanger or wire to fish the rubber band through the second CD. Bend the end of the wire into a small hook and use it to latch onto the free end of the rubber band.

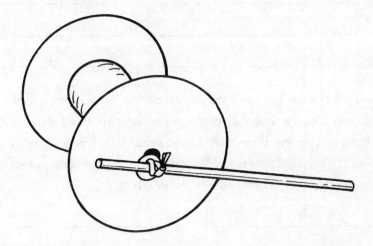

Here is a rubber band racer built from 2 CDs, a toilet paper tube, a rubber band, dowels, and a metal washer.

4. Secure this end of the rubber band with a piece of dowel that is about 5 inches long.

5. Wind up the rubber band with the long dowel, being careful not to break the rubber band. After a couple dozen twists, set the racer on a smooth floor with the long dowel extending beyond the edge of the CD. Release it. If the racer doesn't travel very far, wind up the rubber band more times and release it again.

Name: _____

# Rubber Band Racer

## TEST

Wind up the rubber band and place the CD wheels on the start line of a test track. Release the racer and measure how far it travels in a straight line.

Find the minimum number of twists required to get your racer to move. Record that number in the table below. Then increase the number of twists by 5 and repeat the test, recording the distance in the table. Keep going until the rubber band breaks.

| Number of windings | Distance traveled (units) |
|---|---|
|  |  |
|  |  |
|  |  |
|  |  |
|  |  |
|  |  |

Use graph paper to graph the data you recorded. With no twists of the rubber band, the racer didn't go anywhere, so the graph point (0,0) is a data point. Circle all the data points and connect them with a light pencil line. Use the horizontal axis to represent distance traveled across the floor and the vertical axis to represent how much energy you input. What story does the graph tell? _____

_____

Record the farthest distance your racer traveled on the board, adjacent to your team name. Try to break your record for distance. Try using more than 1 rubber band. Should you loop the rubber bands in a long line (series) or connect each to both dowels (parallel)? Cut larger wheels out of cardboard and see if they affect the distance your racer travels. What else could you try?

## REFLECT

When you increase the number of twists on the rubber band, it stretches. Eventually you reach the "elastic limit" of the rubber band, beyond which it doesn't stretch. Why does the rubber band break?

# Mousetrap Car

## Challenge

Design, build, and test a car powered by a mousetrap that travels as far as possible.

## Overview

Mousetraps provide inexpensive energy storage devices that can power cars and boats. There is a surprising amount of experimentation required to make a good mousetrap car. This activity can last a day or a couple of weeks.

## Materials

Mousetraps (1 per team)
⅛″ brass tubes (12″ per team)
CDs for wheels (4 per team), or wooden wheels (4 per team)
¼″ dowels (12″ per team)
Wood glue
Nylon string (1 ball)
Wood slats, wood veneer sheets, or balsa wood sheets
Small nails (1 per team)
CD wheel inserts (available at http://www.kelvin.com)
Coping saws
Measuring sticks or tapes
Pliers with cutting edge
Hand drill and bits
Stopwatches

## Design Concept

A mousetrap powers a car. As the trap closes, it pulls an extended arm attached to the drive axle with a piece of string.

## The Details

The brass tube allows you to extend the lever arm of the mousetrap, which will result in longer travel distances. Using CDs for the drive wheels results in longer travel distances than using smaller wheels. If you don't have CD wheel inserts (which allow the CDs to mount on ¼-inch dowels), glue small wooden wheels with ¼-inch openings onto the CDs.

Exhibit a completed car to your inventors or merely give them some design hints. The design details are provided here; you decide how much to share.

The length of the brass tube you use determines how long the car will be. When the trap is compressed, the top of the tube (which holds the string connected to the drive axle) should be directly above the drive axle.

The car body must be constructed to withstand the strong force exerted by a mousetrap. On the other hand, the car needs to be as light as possible. Use wood slats (⅜-inch wide) or balsa wood or wood veneer sheets (¼-inch wide). Most cardboard isn't strong enough.

Attach the nondrive wheels with the same approach used in earlier models: use fat straws as bearings. However, the drive wheels have too great a force exerted on them to use this system. Either drill holes through the wood slats or make bearings out of small pieces of wood and glue them to the wood body. Use wood glue and clamp the pieces together while the glue dries.

Alignment is critical as is reducing friction in the bearings. You can insert fat straws in the bearing holes to reduce friction.

Shorten the trap arm by cutting below the ninety-degree bend. This lets you slide the brass tube over the remaining arm to extend it.

Cut the string so it is three inches longer than the length from the tip of the brass tube mounted on the trap to the rear axle. Slide one end of the string into the open end of the brass tube, and crimp the end of the tube with pliers or a vice to hold the string. Tie a loop in the other end of the string.

After you've installed the drive axle, drill a tiny hole though the axle. Push a small nail through the hole and cut the nail with wire cutters or pliers so it sticks out about ⅛-inch above the axle. To secure the string to the drive axle, put the loop of

This mousetrap car uses an extension arm (brass tube) to get a longer pull on the wheels.

string around the nail and wind the wheels until the brass arm is almost touching the axle. Cut away any part of the wood body that rubs against the string while the trap unwinds.

## Getting Started

Consider building and demonstrating a mousetrap car for the class. Before class, establish a track where all testing is to be done. Mark a start line on a smooth floor and provide measuring tools.

## Teachable Moments

Mousetrap cars provide such a rich learning opportunity that you could easily organize a physics program around building them. Instruct students to test their cars in a designated area so you can help teams understand what happens and what they can do to improve their car. For example, if the drive wheels slip on the ground, ask them how they could increase the friction of the wheels and ask them what pickup truck drivers do to increase rear wheel traction. If a car isn't going far, ask them what could be slowing the car down. Friction is the most likely cause—the car may be moving too slowly for air drag to affect its movement.

## References

*Mouse Trap Cars: A Teacher's Guide* (Doc Fizzix Publishing Company, 1998) by Al Balmer is the definitive guide to making and racing these vehicles.

The size of the mousetrap car is determined by the length of the extension arm. The arm should be directly above the drive axle when the spring is fully extended.

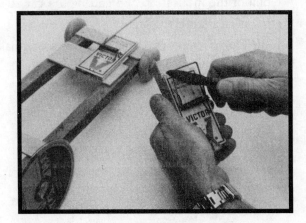

Cut the bail on the mousetrap so the brass tube can slide onto the straight section of metal wire.

# Mousetrap Car

## CHALLENGE

Design, build, and test a car powered by a mousetrap. The goal is to design a car that travels as far as possible.

## DESIGN

Examine the materials available and consider how to build a strong, yet light car body and how to attach wheels. The mousetrap will exert a lot of force on the drive wheels, so they have to be held securely in place.

In order for your car to produce the longest runs possible, you will need to extend the lever arm of the mousetrap. Cut and remove the upper part of the bail (the metal wire that snaps shut on your fingers if you aren't careful) on the mousetrap, leaving 1 arm. Slide a brass tube onto this arm to extend it.

Other design issues include giving the wheels enough friction so they won't slip, connecting the mousetrap to the axle or wheels, holding the axle in place against the pull of the mousetrap, and getting the car to travel in a straight line.

Do you want to use large wheels or small wheels on the drive axle? _____

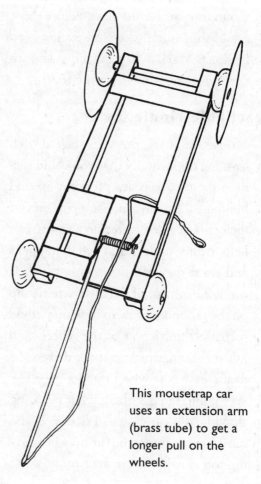

This mousetrap car uses an extension arm (brass tube) to get a longer pull on the wheels.

Name: _____

# Mousetrap Car

## TEST

Take your car to the test track for all testing. Measure the distance the car travels, but record only distances greater than 3 feet. Alter 1 aspect of your design to produce a longer travel time. Record what you changed for each test and change only 1 design feature at a time.

| Test number | Modifications | Distance (units) |
|---|---|---|
| 1 | Initial design (no change) | |
| 2 | | |
| 3 | | |
| 4 | | |
| 5 | | |
| 6 | | |
| 7 | | |

To calculate the speed of your car, measure a distance 5 feet from the start line and put a piece of tape on the floor. With a stopwatch, time how long it takes the car to travel the initial 5 feet. Repeat this experiment twice more and average the times. Use the average time to calculate the car's speed.

| Trial # | Time (seconds) |
|---|---|
| 1 | |
| 2 | |
| 3 | |
| Average | |

The average speed is the distance divided by the average time:

$V = D/T$, where $D = 5$ feet.

Calculate the average speed _____ (units) _____.

Name: _____

# Mousetrap Car

Repeat the previous experiment and calculate the car's speed in the middle of the run, instead of at the start of the run. Estimate where the midpoint of a run will be and set up a 5-feet-long course there. Start the car at the start line and measure the time it takes to cross the new course. Record that time here.

| Trial # | Time (seconds) |
|---------|----------------|
| 1 | |
| 2 | |
| 3 | |
| Average | |

Calculate the average speed _____ (units) _____.

Did the speed change from the first measurement? _____. If it did, why do you think it changed?

_____

_____

_____

_____

_____

_____

_____

Did the car accelerate during the initial part of its run? _____

Name: _____

# Mousetrap Car

## REFLECT

The mousetrap stores energy that you use to power the car. List all the other ways you can think of for storing energy to drive a vehicle.

1. _____

2. _____

3. _____

4. _____

5. _____

6. _____

7. _____

8. _____

9. _____

10. _____

# Springer

## Challenge

Fashion an interesting-looking springer that can fitfully fall down a dowel.

## Overview

This simple toy is fun to make and can facilitate discussions about gravity, energy, and springs. Students can exercise their creativity by adding artistic design elements to their spinger. Upon release, the spinger bobs up and down, sliding down the dowel between bobs.

## Materials

Blocks of wood, use the least expensive fence boards, cut to
  a square shape of 1″ × 4″ (1 per springer)
¼″ dowels, 18″ long, (1 per springer)
Large paper clips
Corks (1 per springer)
Hot glue or white glue
Decorations: plastic eyes, yarn for hair, pipe cleaners for limbs
Hand drill with bits

## Design Concept

The springer is made of a spring wound from a paper clip. It bounces up and down along the dowel, falling only when the coiled spring aligns with the dowel.

## The Details

Wood blocks support a vertical dowel. Wind a large paper clip around the dowel three times, and then open it slightly so it can slide down the dowel. Jam the upper end of the paper clip into the back of a decorated cork.

To launch a springer, slide the cork and paper clip to the top of the dowel and release it. If it doesn't start moving downward, flick the top of the cork with your finger. The cork should spring up and down and each move-

A large paper clip is wound around the dowel, with one end holding the character (cork).

ment should allow the attached paper clip to slide farther down the dowel. Loosen or tighten the paper clip around the dowel to produce the ideal motion.

## Getting Started

Demonstrate a completed springer and show students what materials are available for their use.

## Teachable Moments

As students test their springers, ask them what pulls the springer downward. They should know that the force of gravity pulls it down. Then ask why the springer doesn't fall straight to the bottom, like a ball would if you released it from a similar height. The paper clip catches on the dowel and only slides downward when it isn't rubbing on the dowel. Why does the springer bounce upward? The paper clip acts like a spring. It stores gravitational energy and rebounds when stopped, carrying the springer upward.

## Variations

One of the most memorable toys invented is a spring: the Slinky. Windup cars use springs to store energy, as do jack-in-the-box toys. Challenge your class to design other basic toys that use springs.

Springers bounce up and down as they slide down the shaft.

Name: _____

# Springer

## CHALLENGE

Make and decorate a springer that jumps all the way down a pole.

## DESIGN

Sketch how the spring will attach to the cork and to the pole in your springer.

Name: _____

# Springer

## INSTRUCTIONS FOR INVENTORS

1. Drill a ¼-inch hole in a piece of wood. Insert a dowel into the hole so it stands vertically.
2. Push 1 end of a large paper clip into the cork. **Be careful not to jam the paper clip into your finger or thumb.**
3. Wrap the spring around the dowel 3 times. Pull the springer to the top of the dowel, give it a downward flick with your finger, and see if it travels to the base.

   You may need to tighten or loosen the tension in the spring (which is determined by the number of times the paper clip wire is wrapped around the dowel) to get the springer to work well.

## TEST

Test your springer to see if it consistently travels to the bottom of the pole. When it is working well, try adding weight to the cork—loop a paper clip around the wire supporting the cork. See what impact the weight has on the upward and downward jumps. Add more paper clips and report your findings below.

The springer bounces up and down _____ times to reach the bottom.

Adding 1 paper clip as weight to the springer causes it to bounce up and down _____ times to reach the bottom.

We tried adding more paper clips and found:

| Number of paper clips | Observations |
|---|---|
| | |
| | |
| | |
| | |
| | |
| | |

# Electric Jitter Critter

## Challenge

Design, build, and test a vehicle powered by eccentric motion.

## Overview

Although inefficient, eccentric motions can move models. A motor with an off-center mass on its shaft provides eccentric motion that jerks the vehicle along. Pagers, cell phones, and back massagers have motors that produce eccentric motion. Weights are attached off center to motor shafts to produce vibrations. These vibrations power jitter critters.

## Materials

> Electric motors (1 per team)
> Alligator clip leads
> AA batteries (1 per team)
> Craft sticks
> Paper or styrene bowls or trays
> Wire
> Hot glue
> Soldering iron
> Flat rubber washers, ½″ wide
> Stopwatches

Pager motors are available from several electronic suppliers including Electronic Goldmine (http://www.goldmine-elec.com). These are small motors with the off-center weights attached to the motor shafts. The motor leads are small and too difficult for students to handle, so you will need to solder connections prior to class. Alternatives include using toy motors (available from many science supply houses) and attaching small washers or nuts to the shaft. Securing the weights to the shaft can be a challenge and you don't want them flying off, potentially into someone's eyes. Drill a hole through the metal washer so it will slide onto the motor shaft. Glue it securely or solder it.

## Design Concept

The vibrating motor is firmly attached to a body. One motor lead is soldered to a battery or battery holder. The second lead is an alligator clip lead, cut in half. Sol-

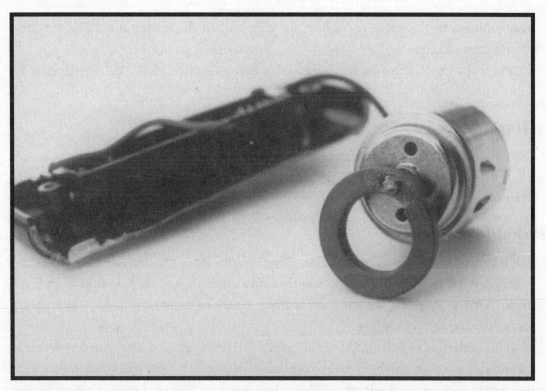

Here is a toy motor with a metal washer glued to its shaft. Connected to a battery, the off-center weight provides jerking motion to the electric jitter critter.

der the bare wire end to the other battery terminal, and clip the alligator end to the motor lead.

## The Details

Secure craft sticks to an inverted paper bowl or styrene tray with hot glue. Also secure the vibrating motor to the top surface with hot glue, using only a tiny dab of glue so you can pull it off later. One motor lead should be soldered to a battery or battery holder. The other motor lead is available to connect to the clip lead.

Tape the AA battery to the top of the jitter critter. With the wire end of the clip

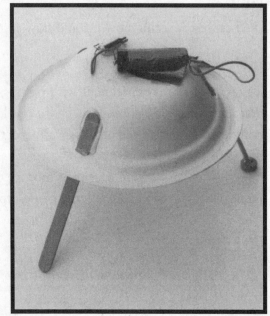

lead soldered to the battery, connect the clip lead to the motor lead. The vibrator should start shaking.

Place the jitter critter on the floor and watch its motion. Now the challenge is to control the motion.

## Getting Started

Demonstrate a working model to launch students into the design phase of the activity. When teams get their jitter critters working, challenge them to race their models against each other.

## Teachable Moments

Ask teams what powers the jitter critters. The motor isn't connected to wheels or a propeller, so what is moving them? Could they make a change to stop or slow the movement (without stopping the motor)? Is there a way to make it move faster without increasing the battery voltage?

The battery is supplying power to move the jitter critters. The kinetic energy is transmitted through the body to the bottom of the legs. As the legs vibrate they jerk the critter forward and backward, but often not in equal amounts. Critical to the motion is having solid connections between the motor and the legs. Insulating the motor's vibrations from the body greatly reduces the motion.

Conclude by having teams race one another across a one-foot-long racetrack.

## Testing

The best test is seeing how far and how fast in a given direction the vehicles can go.

## Variations

Suggest that teams experiment with putting rubber feet on the legs of their jitter critters. They can glue a rubber washer to one leg and test it, and then decide if they want to add rubber feet to the other legs. Instruct them to report the results of these experiments to the class.

Ask the class where eccentric motors could be found. They might suggest cell phones, massage vibrators, electric games, toy trains, cattle prods, and etching devices.

Name: _____

# Electric Jitter Critter

## CHALLENGE

Design, build, and test an electric jitter critter.

## DESIGN

Examine the materials available and consider how your team should assemble its critter. What shape body will you use? How many legs will your jitter critter have? Where will you place them? Where will you locate the motor and battery? Sketch the design below.

Name: _____

# Electric Jitter Critter

## INSTRUCTIONS FOR INVENTORS

See your teacher for guidance on building your jitter critters.

## TEST

When your jitter critter works, place it on a smooth surface and measure the time it takes to travel 1 foot (30 centimeters). Record the time below. Alter your jitter critter design to make it go faster.

| Trial # | Time (seconds) | Speed (units) | Improvements made |
|---------|----------------|---------------|-------------------|
| 1 | | | |
| 2 | | | |
| 3 | | | |
| 4 | | | |
| 5 | | | |

What changes were most effective in improving the speed of your jitter critter?

_____

What changes decreased the speed of your jitter critter?

_____

# Through the Air

Nothing captures the imagination like a flying toy. A disk floating through the air or rocket soaring skyward can seem magical. Understanding that magic is a task for science.

In general, the flying activities in this section require that students measure horizontal distances. This is a more straightforward measurement than a vertical measurement and is easily achieved within the confines of equipment and time.

As we enter the second century of human flight, more attention will be paid to the technological accomplishments of the past one hundred years. Student writing projects should connect with the hands-on activities. Here are some suggested subjects:

Alan Adler, inventor of the Aerobie

Alexander Graham Bell, builder of giant kites

George Cayley, father of aerodynamics who discovered "lift"

Glenn Curtiss, inventor of the aileron

Lawrence Hargrave, inventor of the box kite

Otto Lilienthal, first person to fly a glider

Joseph Michael and Jacques Ètienne Montgolfier, inventors
    of the first hot-air balloon capable of carrying humans

Fred Morrison, inventor of the Frisbee

Igor Sikorksy, inventor of the helicopter

Orville and Wilbur Wright, inventors of the first heavier-
    than-air, powered airplane

Two sources of information on these inventors on the Internet are National Inventors Hall of Fame (http://www.invent.org) and the National Toy Hall of Fame (http://www.strongmuseum.org/NTHoF/NTHoF.html).

# Gravity Ball Launcher

## Challenge

Build and test a launcher that uses momentum transferred from a basketball to launch smaller balls.

## Overview

In this project, the gravity ball launcher will produce amazingly high launches that erupt from a tin can taped to a basketball. Student teams will experiment to maximize the height of a launched ball. This is an outdoor or gymnasium activity.

## Materials

Basketballs (1 per team)

Tin cans with both ends removed (1 per team)

Variety of balls that fit into the tin cans, including ping-pong balls, super balls, tennis balls, and racket balls. **Don't use golf balls** as they can cause damage.

Duct tape

Means of measuring height of launched balls (tape measure, yard stick, etc.)

## Design Concept

Tape a tin can to a basketball with duct tape. The can will be used to hold smaller balls in place while a student drops the basketball from a constant height. Dropped from three feet above the ground, a basketball can launch a tennis ball fifteen to twenty feet.

## Getting Started

Demonstrate how a gravity ball launcher works. Drop one tennis ball into a tin can that is securely taped to a basketball. Holding the can so the open end is pointed upward, drop the basketball from chest height. Upon impact with the floor, the basketball will transfer much of its momentum to the tennis ball, which will fly out at great speed.

The gravity ball launcher can propel a small ball several times the drop height of the basketball launcher.

96

Repeat the experiment while standing in front of a wall so students can gauge how high the basketball rebounds. Instruct them to focus on the basketball so they can report its rebound height. Measure the height of the rebound according to their observations. Repeat the experiment a third time, but now do not put the tennis ball in the can. Ask the students what they expect to happen.

Without the tennis ball in the can, the basketball rebounds off the floor significantly higher. Provided that you dropped the basketball from the same height each time, why would it rebound to different heights? What was different in the last two experiments?

Upon impact some of the momentum (mass times velocity) and kinetic energy (mass times velocity squared) of the basketball are transferred to the tennis ball. Both the basketball and tennis ball travel at the same speed on the way down, but upon collision the transfer of momentum increases the smaller balls' upward velocity up to three times its downward velocity. Tripling the velocity raises the resulting height nine fold.

Here is a gravity ball launcher with two balls inside a metal can.

Of course a student may want to try putting two balls in the launcher. Provided the top ball has a smaller mass than the ball below, it can climb to fifty times its original drop height (Walker, 1977).

Emphasize that only gravity launches will be permitted. There is to be no throwing the balls at the ground.

## Teachable Moments

As teams are testing launchers, ask them individually where the smaller ball gets the energy to fly. If they recognize that the smaller ball gets energy from the larger ball, ask how they could observe if the larger ball transfers all the energy possible to the smaller ball. What changes would they expect to see if they were able to extract more energy from the larger ball? (The larger ball would rebound to lower heights. If all of its energy and momentum were transferred to the smaller ball, it wouldn't rebound at all). So one measure of success in this activity is how low a larger ball rebounds.

Estimating the height of the flying balls is an exercise in mathematics that you can ask your students to undertake. Teams could make inclinometers (a straw taped to the bottom of a protractor for sighting and a weight on a string to indicate the vertical) or could compare the height to some reference.

*Note:* An Astro-Blaster is a science toy that uses this concept to launch a small ball. You can see the toy and read the manufacturer's description of how it works at http://www.fascinations.com/Astro.htm.

# Gravity Ball Launcher

## CHALLENGE

Build and test a ball launcher that uses only gravity as the driving force. Design a launcher that sends a ball as high possible.

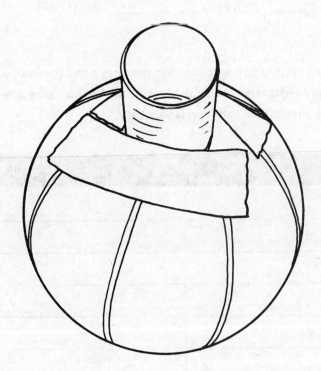

The gravity ball launcher can propel a small ball several times the drop height of the basketball launcher.

Experiment with different combinations of balls. Record how different balls rebound. Estimate how high the balls fly. You could perform the experiment in front of a wall and estimate height by counting the number of bricks or blocks. Describe how you will measure the height of the ball:

_____

_____

Name: _____

# Gravity Ball Launcher

## INSTRUCTIONS FOR INVENTORS

Pick 1 height to use for dropping the launcher in each experiment. You could use the height of 1 team member's shoulder or waist. Measure that height and record it here. Drop height is _____(units) _____.

### Two-Ball Drops

Indicate below what type of ball you used for the larger ball (basketball) and smaller ball, and record the height achieved by the smaller ball. It may take a few drops before you get one where the smaller ball travels vertically.

| Larger ball | Smaller ball | Height achieved by smaller ball (units) |
|---|---|---|
|  |  |  |
|  |  |  |
|  |  |  |
|  |  |  |
|  |  |  |

What combination of balls gave you the highest launch?

_____

Use this combination in the next experiment.

# Gravity Ball Launcher

## Three-Ball Drops

Use the combination of the larger ball (basketball) and the smaller ball that produced the highest launches in the 2-ball experiments and add a second small ball. Try different small balls in this combination.

| Top ball | Height (units) |
|---|---|
|  |  |
|  |  |
|  |  |
|  |  |
|  |  |

What combination of balls gave the highest launches?

_____

## REFLECT

What factors (size, weight, construction, etc.) of a ball determined how high it would fly? _____

Did you try 2 identical balls? What happened?

_____

_____

_____

Name: _____

# Gravity Ball Launcher

Design a launcher that could reliably drop 4 or more balls. Sketch it here.

Could NASA launch a spacecraft using this method? How would it work? Would you want to ride in the spacecraft? _____

_____

# Flying Saucer

## Challenge

Build and test a flying saucer and a ring that travels as far as possible.

## Overview

After a brief introduction on how spinning plates fly, launch students into self-directed discovery.

## Materials

Sturdy paper plates (4–5 per team)
Masking tape
Scissors
Metal washers (8–10 per team)
Drawing compass
Hot glue
Cardboard
Scissors
Measuring tape or stick
Frisbees and Aerobies

## Design Concept

Although you can use flat cardboard to make a flying saucer, it is easier and faster to start with a paper plate. In order to get most plates to fly, you must increase their aerodynamic drag or add weights. Bending the lip of a plate can greatly increase its drag, as can taping two plates together. Try a variety of configurations of two or more plates. Adding weights (small metal washers or large paper clips) along the outer edges improves the plate's spin and helps balance the lifting forces at the leading edge.

Two or more paper plates can make a great flying saucer.

## Getting Started

Demonstrate the flight of a flat circle of cardboard. Cut a circle twelve to eighteen inches in diameter from corrugated cardboard. Fling it like you would fling a Frisbee.

Tossing the cardboard disk with your right hand will cause the right side to rise in flight, sending it crashing down to the left. Reversing the tossing hand will reverse the side that rises. Ask the class what they can infer about flight from this experiment. Clearly, spin impacts flight characteristics.

Try launching the cardboard disk without spin. Hold both hands on the rear edge and push your hands forward sharply. Immediately the leading edge will rise, the disk will spin and fall to the ground. Ask the class what happened. Clearly there was so much lift on the leading edge that the disk flew upward, stalled, and crashed.

Now demonstrate the flight of a Frisbee. It flies level. Why doesn't it crash to one side like the disk? The answer lies in the shape of the Frisbee. Look at how deep the Frisbee is. It presents a large surface area that pushes air out of the way. It has huge drag that counteracts the lift at the leading edge. Another result of the drag is that the Frisbee can't fly very far.

Commercially made flying saucers achieve balanced flight by having a blunt leading edge (Frisbee) or having a slender leading edge with a lip (Aerobie).

To fly really far, a flying toy must have reduced drag. Demonstrate an Aerobie. Compare the depth of its leading edge to that of a Frisbee. The Aerobie has a tiny fraction of the Frisbee's area and this allows it to fly many times farther than a Frisbee.

But why doesn't the Aerobie crash to one side like the cardboard disk? Look closely at the upper surface. (It helps to cut through one wing of an Aerobie to see the profile). The leading edge rises to a sharp peak, falls into a broad valley, and rises again. This unique (and patented) shape eliminates some of the lift, preventing it from crashing sideways.

Why does lift at a disk's leading edge cause it to crash to one side? For spinning objects, forces applied at one point manifest themselves ninety degrees down spin. Lift at the leading edge shows up on the side of the disk spinning forward, which is why it crashes on opposite sides when thrown with opposing hands.

You can demonstrate this with a spinning bike wheel or even a spinning quarter. Blow on a quarter spinning on a table and, although it will move in the direction you blew, it will also move to one side. The side depends on which direction you spun the coin. Turning a corner on a bike is easy even without holding the handlebars: lean in the direction you want to turn. The bike doesn't fall over in that direction. Instead the front wheel turns in that direction. The force shows up ninety degrees down spin of where it was applied. You applied force at the top of the wheel and the force affected the front of the wheel.

If a spinning flying toy crashes to the left with a right-hand fling, it has too much lift. If it crashes to the right with a right-hand fling, the drag is too great.

## Testing

Instruct students to work in pairs. They should toss their flying saucers to their partners through a safe flight path. The challenge is to throw and catch the saucer with the widest possible distance between partners. After a successful catch, teams measure this separation distance.

## Teachable Moments

There is a great temptation to make several changes at once to a flying saucer. As you circulate among the flight engineers, remind them to change one characteristic at a time and to test it and record their findings. Otherwise they won't discover what design modifications cause the results they see.

## Variations

Use a compass to draw a circle on a plate and cut the circle out. The paper ring can become a model Aerobie. Students can modify it to fly or can combine it with uncut paper plates to create a hybrid flying craft.

Name: _____

# Flying Saucer

## CHALLENGE

Build and test a flying saucer. For your flying toy to be a success, it must fly level as far as possible.

## DESIGN

Picture in your mind what a flying saucer should look like. Is that picture similar to a frisbee or other flying toy? What design characteristics (size, shape,) does it have?

## INSTRUCTIONS FOR INVENTORS

Start with a single paper plate. Fling it toward your partner and record what happens. Then make changes to improve its flight characteristics.

| Experiment # | Describe flight, including measurement of flight distance (units) | What modifications will you make? |
|---|---|---|
| 1 | Initial fling | |
| 2 | | |
| 3 | | |
| 4 | | |
| 5 | | |
| 6 | | |
| 7 | | |
| 8 | | |

## REFLECT

Describe the design of your best flying saucer.

_____

What modifications contributed the most to extending the distance you could fling the saucer? _____

Can you invent an improved Frisbee? Describe it.

# Catapult

## Challenge

Design, build, and test a catapult that launches ping-pong balls as far as possible.

## Overview

Launching a ping-pong ball across a room is inherently inviting and fun. It's also fun to launch a ball as far as possible, so students will be naturally driven to experiment and improve their catapults.

## Materials

This design uses the same materials that the land vehicles use: a large wooden wheel and dowels. These materials allow for testing a variety of lengths of throwing arms and designs for the body of the catapult.

More durable models can be made using ¼-inch plywood for sides and a one-inch by two-inch furring strip for the base. The wooden model takes longer to build but provides great learning opportunities in cutting, drilling, and assembling the wood pieces.

Large cereal boxes (1 per team)
Wooden wheels, 2″ diameter with ¼″ center hole (1 per team)
¼″ dowels (18″ per team)
Paper egg carton
Variety of rubber bands
Hot glue
Ping-pong balls (1 per team)
Masking tape
Measuring tape
Safety goggles
Wire cutters
Hand drill and ¼″ bit
Scissors
Hole punch
Vice

## Design Concept

Drilling a hole in the edge of a wooden wheel provides a place to insert the throwing arm. The wheel, with a dowel placed through its center, rotates in the holes punched in the sides of the cereal box.

## The Details

To make the base for the catapult, cut a cereal box in half along a diagonal, starting about two-thirds of the way up one side of the box. Use one half as the base and use the other half (cut to fit) to reinforce the base. Jam the second half into the first half and tape them together.

Locate the axle about half way along the diagonal cut. Starting at the midpoint on the diagonal, move half way to the front corner of the boxes and punch a hole. Make a corresponding hole in the other cardboard side.

To make the throwing arm, drill a ¼-inch hole into the edge of a wheel. Place the wheel in a vice—don't try to hold it by hand. Cut a section of dowel (four to six inches long) and slide it into the hole. Don't glue this; you want to be able to change throwing arms to test which produces the longest launches.

The cup that holds one egg in a paper egg carton fits a ping-pong ball perfectly and will serve as a basket. Attach the basket to the outboard end of the dowel and glue it in place.

Slide a five-inch piece of dowel through the hole in one side of the catapult, through the wheel, and through the hole in the other side. To construct a more advanced catapult, add two short sections of a fat straw on either side of the wheel to hold it in the center of the box.

A cereal box catapult can fling a ping-pong ball ten to fifteen feet.

Add two more pieces of dowel. One anchors the rubber band—a two-inch piece of dowel will work. The other stops the throwing arm; it needs to be four to six inches long.

For the stop, punch pairs of holes with a hole punch along the edge of the diagonal in front of the axle. Slide the longer dowel through one pair. You can adjust the distance and the trajectory by moving this dowel to other places.

Cut a hole in the small vertical panel of the base large enough to slide a rubber band through it. Secure the rubber band by looping one end around the short piece of dowel. Twist the rubber band several times to prevent it from sliding off the wheel. Loop the free end around the throwing arm. You're ready to launch. Students can experiment with different lengths of rubber band (or by looping two or more together) and different placements of the anchor on the front panel.

## Getting Started

Have teams sketch how they might launch a ping-pong ball. Then, show them a model you made to demonstrate how a catapult works and give them more ideas.

Set up a test area where they can launch ping-pong balls safely. Point out that anyone shooting rubber bands or anything else at a person, animal, or breakable object will not be allowed to participate in the catapult building and testing.

## Teachable Moments

Students engage in the scientific process of discovery as they try a variety of solutions to address the problems of their catapult designs. They must break down a problem into its component pieces and try solutions for each. Forces and energy are concepts embedded in the project. Ask questions about the results of stretching rubber bands ("To launch the ball farther, how far do you pull back on the rubber band?") to introduce the concept of Hooke's Law (the force of a spring or elastic material is proportional to the distance it's stretched). You can also point out that the rubber band serves the same purpose as a battery in an electric vehicle: both store energy and release it when needed.

Rubber bands store energy for these catapults. Ask students to think of other physical and chemical energy storage devices. Examples include springs and dams for physical storage, and batteries and coal for coal-fired electric plants for chemical storage.

Name: _____

# Catapult

## CHALLENGE

Design, build, and test a catapult that will fling a ping-pong ball as far as possible.

## DESIGN

If you had only 1 rubber band, what simple device could you build to launch a ping-pong ball across the room? Sketch your designs below.

Look at the materials that are available and consider how you could use them. Then work with your teammates to build a catapult.

Name: _____

# Catapult

## INSTRUCTIONS FOR INVENTORS

1.  To make the base of the catapult, cut a cereal box in half along a diagonal, starting about ⅔ of the way up 1 side of the box. Use one half as the base and use the other half (cut to fit) to reinforce the base. Fit the second half into the first half and tape them together.

2.  Locate the axle about half way along the diagonal cut. Starting at the midpoint on the diagonal, move half way to the front corner of the boxes and punch a hole. Make a corresponding hole in the other cardboard side.

3.  To make the throwing arm, drill a ¼-inch hole into the edge of a wheel. Place the wheel in a vice—don't try to hold it by hand. Cut a section of dowel (4–6 inches long) to slide into the hole. Don't glue this; you want to be able to change throwing arms to test which produces the longest launches.

4.  The cup that holds 1 egg in a paper egg carton fits a ping-pong ball perfectly to serve as a basket. Attach the basket to the outboard end of the dowel and glue it in place.

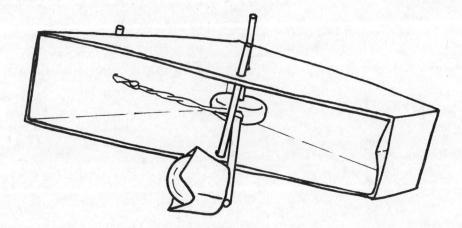

A cereal box catapult can fling a ping-pong ball 10–15 feet.

# Catapult

5.  Slide a 5-inch piece of dowel through the hole in 1 side of the catapult, through the wheel, and through the hole in the other side. To construct a more advanced catapult, add 2 short sections of a fat straw on either side of the wheel to hold it in the center of the box.

6.  Add 2 more pieces of dowel. One anchors the rubber band—a 2-inch piece of dowel will work. The other stops the throwing arm; it needs to be 4–6 inches long.

7.  For the stop, punch pairs of holes with a hole punch along the edge of the diagonal in front of the axle. Slide the longer dowel through one pair. You can adjust the distance and the trajectory by moving this dowel to other places.

8. Cut a hole in the small vertical panel of the base large enough to slide a rubber band through it. Secure the rubber band by looping 1 end around the short piece of dowel. Twist the rubber band several times to prevent it from sliding off the wheel. Loop the free end around the throwing arm. You're ready to launch.

# Catapult

## TEST

Make sure you aim your catapult so the ping-pong balls don't hit anyone or anything except the floor. **Anyone who hits another person, an animal, or a breakable object will be removed from this activity. Wear safety goggles when launching the catapult.**

Hold the base of your catapult on the start line with one hand and pull the throwing arm back with the other hand. Have a teammate load a ping-pong ball into the basket. When there is no one in the ball's flight path, release your grip on the arm.

Measure from the start line to the point where the ball first hits the floor (not where it rolls or bounces). Record this distance below.

First design:

| Launch number | Distance ball traveled in the air |
|---|---|
| 1 | |
| 2 | |
| 3 | |
| Average | |

Name: _____

# Catapult

How could you increase the range of the catapult? Watch the throwing arm as you launch a ball and decide if you should change the length of the throwing arm, the position of the rubber band, the place where the throwing arm stops, or something else.

Record what changes you make and what impact they have on the distance the ball travels. Subtract the average distance determined in your prior calculation from the distance the ball travels with these innovations. A positive number will be an improvement in distance.

| Design changes | Impact (distance ball travels) |
|---|---|
|  |  |
|  |  |
|  |  |
|  |  |

## REFLECT

Stretching and releasing the rubber band is an example of a physical reaction in which energy is stored and released. Other types of energy-releasing reactions are chemical and nuclear. List devices and materials that release stored energy in physical, chemical, and nuclear reactions.

| Physical | Chemical | Nuclear |
|---|---|---|
| Rubber bands | Gasoline engine | The sun |
|  |  |  |
|  |  |  |

# Trebuchet

## Challenge

Design, build, and test a gravity-powered catapult to launch a golf ball as far as possible.

## Overview

It is amazing how far you can fling a ball using a falling weight. In the Middle Ages, trebuchets launched the profession of engineering and ended the era of castles as innovative individuals perfected this mechanism to pitch heavy stone balls in the air and knock holes in castle walls. To undertake this activity you need a space in which golf balls can fly twenty to twenty-five feet without damaging things or injuring people.

## Materials

Corrugated cardboard boxes (1 per team)
¼" dowels (36" per team)
Fat straws (1 per team)
Wooden wheels, 2" diameter (1 per team)
Golf balls (1 per team)
2 lbs scuba weights or plastic bottles with 2 pints of water (1 weight per team)
String
Screw eyes (1 per team)
Small nails (1 per team)
Heavy-duty scissors for cutting cardboard
Hand drill with ¼" bit
Hot glue
Measuring stick or tape
Wire cutters

## Design Concept

A falling weight attached to the short end of a lever arm spins a projectile into an arc. The projectile is connected to the long end of a lever arm by a string that serves as a sling. The sling releases the projectile at the optimal point along the arc to give the maximum length trajectory.

Or not. It's difficult to tune a trebuchet so it produces successful launches. Hernando Cortez supposedly built a trebuchet to attack the Aztec capital, but its first and only launch pitched the projectile straight up in the air. The projectile destroyed the trebuchet upon landing. Be prepared for golf balls to fly in any direction.

## The Details

The arm supporting the weight should be about one-quarter the length of the arm flinging the ball. The exact size will depend on the size of the box you use for the base. In the trebuchet shown here, the throwing arm is 20 inches long and the weight arm is 5.5 inches long.

Drill ¼-inch holes into the edge of a two-inch wooden wheel to support each arm. Drill the holes on opposite sides of the wheel. Insert the dowels into these holes. Glue the dowels unless you want to experiment with different lengths.

To reduce friction, run the axle through sections of fat straw that fit snugly in the sides of the box. Glue the straws in place.

The ball should rest inside the base in a trough made of cardboard so it doesn't roll to one side. To attach the golf ball, drill a small hole through it and pass one end of a thirty-six-inch-long string through the hole. Tie the string to itself to hold the ball. Cut the string to a length so the golf ball can sit beneath the axle when it is in the trough. The end of the string should touch the end of the throwing arm with several inches to spare. Tie several loops with overhand knots in the end of the string. Each loop provides an attachment point, so having several allows you to adjust the length of the sling (string) by using different loops.

Tap a small nail in the end of the flinging arm and cut off the nail's head with wire cutters. Place one of the string's loops over this nail.

The trebuchet can launch a golf ball twenty-five feet using two to three pounds of weight.

In a trebuchet, a screw eye in the end of the weight arm allows you to add weights easily.

Screw in a small screw eye in the end of the weight arm. You can loop the weight (using a twist tie or string holding the weight) onto the screw eye.

Launch the projectile. **These trebuchets can fling a ball a long distance in either direction, forward or backward. Check around you to make sure you're not near anything breakable. A good trebuchet, using two pounds, will launch a golf ball twenty feet.**

Roll the golf ball into the trough while placing a loop of string over the nail. Pick up the back of the base to keep the golf ball from rolling back out.

One team member can attach the weight, while another supports the weight so it doesn't pull down the arm. Lower the base to the ground and release the weight so it can fall.

The next step involves tuning the trebuchet. If the ball goes straight up or backward, it is being released too early. Use a longer section of string. (Now the loops come in handy as they allow you to adjust the length of the string.)

Conversely, if the ball flings downward in front of the trebuchet, the ball is releasing too late. Shorten the string.

If no adjustment of the string gives a satisfying fling, increase the weight by 2.5–3 pounds.

## Getting Started

Show students a working model that they can copy. They will need to observe several launches in order to understand how this machine works.

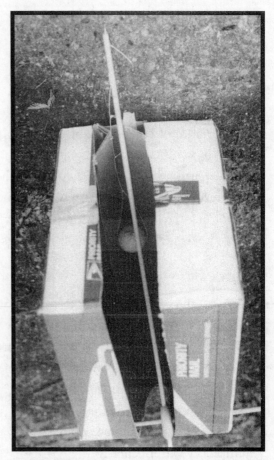

The golf ball rests in a trough inside the trebuchet. Loops in the string make it easy to test different string lengths.

A scuba dive weight is attached to the throwing arm.

Set up a safe launch area where flying golf balls won't break anything or land on innocent bystanders.

## Teachable Moments

The technology of trebuchets is not terribly important for students to learn; however the experience of solving engineering problems and the fun of flinging make this a great activity.

Ask questions to help team members hone in on the technical problems they are encountering, especially when tuning their trebuchets. Where does the energy come from to fling the balls? What force (gravity) launches the ball? Challenge the teams to improve their model to get longer launches.

## References

NOVA produced an excellent program on trebuchets (*Secrets of Lost Empires 2: Medieval Siege*). Less technical, but loads of fun, is the *Northern Exposure* episode in which Chris launches a piano with a giant trebuchet (episode 3.14: "Burning Down the House": http://home.comcast.net/~mcnotes/mcnotes.html#video). There are many Web pages that show homemade trebuchets of substantial size:

http://www.pbs.org/wgbh/nova/lostempires/trebuchet/
http://www.siege-engine.com
http://www.trebuchet.com

# Trebuchet

## CHALLENGE

Make a trebuchet that can launch a golf ball as far as possible using a 2-pound weight.

## DESIGN

Get design ideas by examining the model built by your design chief (teacher) or searching the Web for sites that feature homemade trebuchets. Try http://www.tre-buchet.com/plans.html or http://www.ripcord.ws/plans/plans.html.

The idea is to use a falling weight to fling a ball. Sounds simple, but trebuchets take careful engineering and experimenting. The ball is attached with a length of string to form a sling. To get the pivot arm to rotate, mount it in the side of a wood wheel. An axle (short piece of dowel) supports the wheel from each side and is itself supported by the sides of a cardboard box. On the classroom model, measure the length of the throwing arm and compare it to the length of the arm that supports the weights. You'll want your arms to have about the same proportions. Measure the length of the string and use that as a guide when cutting your string. Check out how the ends of the string are attached to the throwing arm. The string has to stay on the arm until the ball is in the right position for release.

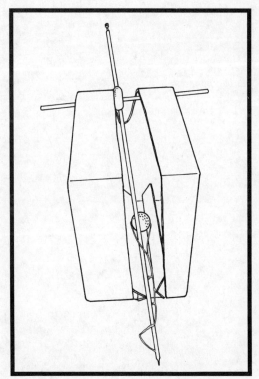

## TEST

Make sure that no one will be injured and nothing will be damaged by the golf ball before launching it. Check for people and objects in front of and behind the tre-buchet, as the golf ball could go in either direction.

Measure the distance from the base of your trebuchet to the final resting spot of the golf ball. List the modifications you made for each launch. While measuring, make sure you don't walk in front of another team that is preparing to launch.

The golf ball rests in a trough inside the tre-buchet. Loops in the string make it easy to test different string lengths.

Name: _____

# Trebuchet

| Modifications made | Launch distance (units) |
|---|---|
| Initial launch | |
| | |
| | |
| | |
| | |
| | |
| | |

Name: _____

# Trebuchet

## REFLECT

What design features of a trebuchet are most important in producing a long launch?

1. _____

2. _____

3. _____

4. _____

List the simple machines that are used in a trebuchet. If you're not sure what a simple machine is, research the Web for information. A good site to check is http://www.mos.org/sln/Leonardo/InventorsToolbox.html.

# Straw Rocket

## Challenge

Build and test different rocket designs to achieve the maximum range.

## Overview

This is such an engaging activity that kids would do it without being told. They use their lung power to launch rockets. Although the bigger lungs may launch an object farther, rocket design is critical to success.

## Materials

> Fat straws (at least 1 per person)
> Regular straws (at least 1 per person)
> Masking tape
> Paper clips
> Scissors
> Measuring tape or meter stick

## Design Concept

Fat straws form the rocket fuselage and regular straws are the launchers. Successful designs will include an airtight nose, small fins for control, and possibly weight (paper clips) on the nose. These launches will occur near the optimal angle of forty-five degrees.

## The Details

Each student can make his or her own rocket and launcher. To seal the rocket and make it airtight, bend the tip of one end of a fat straw over itself and tape it in place. Blow through the straw to check if it's airtight. Don't share any other details of design; instead, let students discover them.

Slide this basic fuselage onto a regular straw, which serves as a launcher. With a mighty blast from your lungs, launch the fat straw rocket. It will travel a few meters with wobbly flight.

Most straw rockets without fins will travel twenty feet at most. Adding fins will allow them to achieve much greater launch ranges. However, adding very large fins will result in shorter flights. To make a simple fin, use a piece of masking tape about one inch long. Fold the tape in half so the center of the tape sticks to itself and leaves short sections at each end that aren't stuck together. Use the two free ends of the tape to attach the fin to the base (opposite end from the closed end). Additional fins can be added on the other sides. Trim each fin with scissors to construct the smallest size that controls flight.

Experiment with adding weight, either in the form of masking tape or a paper clip attached to the nose of the rocket. The beauty of this activity is that innovations can be tested in seconds, so encourage students to perform as many trials as time allows.

## Getting Started

Have students envision what a rocket should look like, possibly drawing ideas on the board. After they make their rockets, ask them to estimate how far (in meters or feet) they think their rocket will travel. Have them record that estimated distance on the board and later compare it to what they achieved.

## Teachable Moments

Some students will put wings on their rockets or will place fins higher on the fuselage. Ask them what their rockets did in flight. Ask them to picture a NASA rocket and compare that image to the rockets they made. Most kids will recognize that rockets have fins (small, winglike structures at the base of the rocket) and planes have wings (larger structures, usually located near the center of gravity, that provide lift). Planes use lift to fly, but

rockets don't. Rockets don't fly per se; they power their way through the air. Fins provide drag so the back of the rocket stays behind the front of the rocket, supplying directional stability.

When students are about to launch, ask them what launch angle will achieve the farthest distance. Most kids instinctively know that the angle midway between the vertical to horizontal planes (forty-five degrees) will give the best launch. If they give this answer, ask them what angle they are describing, measured in degrees. If they don't know which launching angle works best, ask if it would be to angle straight up (ninety degrees) or directly forward (zero degrees). If neither of these works well, ask what other angles could improve the rocket's distance.

## Testing

Provide a way for students to measure their launches. Place masking tape markers on the floor and have students measure the distance from these markers to the landing point. Instruct them to measure and record each launch.

## Variations

Students can make rockets out of paper instead of fat straws. Direct them to rip office paper into thirds, lengthwise. Roll one-third around a pencil and tape it into a cylinder. This makes a good straw substitute.

# Straw Rocket

## CHALLENGE

Build and test a straw rocket. Find the design that allows your rocket to travel as far as possible.

## DESIGN

Think about what a real rocket looks like, and then visualize a design that transforms a fat straw into a rocket. Perform a test launch and record the distance below. To improve the distance the rocket travels, make one change each time you launch the rocket and record both the distance and the change.

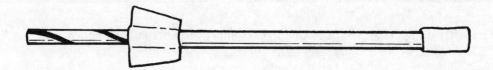

A regular straw is the launcher and a fat straw is the rocket. Masking tape holds the folded end (nose) closed and forms fins at the other end.

How can you make the rocket or any of its parts

Bigger? _____

Smaller? _____

Lighter? _____

Heavier? _____

Name: _____

# Straw Rocket

| Changes made | Distance traveled (units) |
|---|---|
| Initial design | |
| | |
| | |
| | |
| | |
| | |

List what design changes made the biggest improvements in your rocket:

_____

_____

_____

_____

_____

# Pneumatic Blast Rocket

## Challenge

Improve the basic design of a paper rocket so it travels as far as possible (over 150 feet).

## Overview

These rockets are made of scrap office paper, tape, and paper clips. Kids launch them by jumping onto an empty two-liter bottle connected to a launch tube. There are no explosives or combustibles and kids get a visceral feel for the energy required to launch the rocket. Although they are called rockets here, these aren't technically rockets because they don't have an onboard motor and energy source.

## Materials

> 2-liter soda bottles (5–6 per team)
> Bike inner tube
> PVC pipe, ¾″, schedule 200
> 8.5″ × 11″ office paper
> Index cards or business cards (1 pack)
> Masking tape
> Paper clips
> Duct tape
> Scissors
> Hacksaw
> For the launcher:
>> Pine board, 6″ long
>> 2″ × 4″ stud for support feet
>> 2″ long bolt, two nuts, and two washers
>> Hot glue
>> Drill and bits
>> Protractor

## Design Concept

This is a homemade version of the popular "Stomp Rocket." However, this version flies farther and allows students to make design changes to improve their rockets' flight characteristics. The launcher design allows students to measure the angle of launch so they can compare it to the distance that real rockets fly.

## The Details

The simplest launcher connects a sixteen-inch length of the PVC pipe to a two-liter soda bottle with a length of bicycle inner tube. I collect the inner tubes that bike stores discard and make sure the sections I use don't have holes. Stretch one end of the inner tube over the mouth of two-liter bottle and hold it in place with masking tape. Although duct tape would hold the inner tube more securely, it's a pain to peel off when you've destroyed the bottle and need to replace it with a new one. Do use duct tape to secure the other end of the inner tube to the PVC pipe.

To allow students to measure the launch angle, mount the launch tube on an upright pine plank. Spray mount a photocopy of a protractor to the plank. Drill a hole through the center of the base of the protractor photo so you can pass a bolt through it. Drill a corresponding hole in a two-inch or larger diameter section of PVC pipe and bolt it in place. Glue the launch tube to the inside of the larger tube and hold it until the glue sets.

To make the rocket fuselage, roll a piece of scrap office paper around the outside of a ten-inch piece of the ¾-inch PVC pipe. Loosen the paper so the pipe slides easily through it. To keep the paper from unrolling, tape the edge of the paper with three short pieces of masking tape. You've just made the fuselage of a rocket

To make the fuselage airtight, you need to fold one end over and tape it in place. Hold one end of the fuselage (the paper cylinder) between your thumbs and middle fingers and pinch inward with your index fingers.

Just before your index fingers touch, pinch your thumbs together with your middle fingers to shut the tube. Tape this with a one-inch piece of masking tape. It's not yet airtight, so fold the end over and tape it down against the fuselage.

The pneumatic blast rocket launcher uses a photocopy of a protractor to facilitate students' measuring the launch angle.

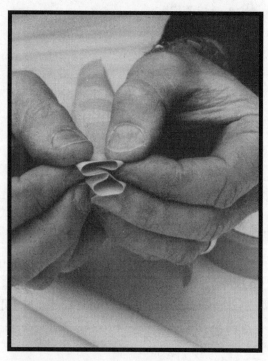

After rolling a sheet of paper around the PVC pipe, close one end by pinching with your index fingers and then collapsing with your thumbs and middle fingers.

The fuselage is now airtight. You can test it by blowing into the end of the tube. No air escapes, so the fuselage is ready.

Launch the rocket. Point the rocket safely down range and away from people and animals. Students should ask a friend to jump on the two-liter bottle with one foot. The target for the foot is the middle of the bottle. Jumping on the end of the bottle or jumping with both feet will destroy the two-liter bottle. Breaking a soon-to-be-recycled two-liter bottle is no problem, except it will take a few minutes to replace it with a new one. To recharge the bottle, blow hard into the end of the launch tube. **If several people will be recharging the bottle, have antiseptic disposable wipes handy to wipe the tube and prevent transmission of germs.**

If several students are launching and retrieving rockets at the same time, ask an adult to direct traffic to minimize the possibility of someone being hit. You may want everyone to wear safety goggles.

## Getting Started

Make one or more launchers and recruit some parent volunteers to help. Establish a safe flight zone either outside on an athletic field or park or inside a

Here is a rocket ready to launch.

Launch the rocket by jumping onto the two-liter soda bottle.

gym. Mark the start line, pace off distances, and mark them every ten feet or so. This will speed up measuring the distances of each launch as teams can measure from these markers.

Show students how to make and launch a fuselage. Demonstrate that the basic fuselage will fly only about thirty feet. Then it hits an invisible wall of air. Actually, the fuselage topples in flight so it flies sideways, encountering much more air resistance than it would if it continued to fly nose first. A few tricks to make a rocket travel far include adding optimally sized and placed fins, a nose cone, and weights (paper clips).

## Teachable Moments

Station yourself by the launcher so you can raise questions about every launch. The most important question to ask is, "What happened?" In general, kids won't be able to answer this question the first or even second time you ask. People won't understand scientific concepts if they can't report the outcomes of an experiment. So developing the skills of observation and reporting is paramount. Don't let students off the hook without giving you an accurate answer. If they can't answer, direct them to repeat the launch, telling them that you'll ask this question again immediately after the launch.

The second most important learning goal of this experiment is to help students associate a cause with the observed effect. Ask them why the rocket behaved as it did. Insist that they point to something on the rocket (although the effect could be associated with environmental conditions or the launcher) that could have caused the effect. Then ask them how they could test the rocket to find out if their hypothesis is correct. The next experiment they run should test this hypothesis.

As the students come up with ideas on what to test next, insist that they test one design change at a time. Otherwise, they won't know which change delivered the result.

Here is a table of effects and possible causes.

| Effects | Possible causes |
| --- | --- |
| The rocket spirals in flight. | Fins are set at an angle to the direction of flight. |
| The rocket goes a short distance and flutters to the ground. | The rocket needs fins or the end isn't sealed shut. |
| The rocket with fins doesn't go far. | The fins may be too large. |
| The fins may be placed too high on the rocket. | They need to be at the base. |
| The rocket may be too light (add paperclips to the nose). | The rocket may need a symmetric nose cone. |
| The rocket veers to one side. | The rocket needs a symmetric nose cone. |

If teams don't come up with the solutions of adding fins or a nose cone to the rocket, ask them to sketch a rocket that they've seen. Ask them what design features the real rocket has that their model rocket doesn't have.

Students often call fins "wings." Point out that wings on a plane provide lift to keep the plane in the air. Fins provide drag to keep a rocket from tumbling and keep it pointed in the right direction. Fins and wings are not the same.

## Testing

Direct teams to innovate their designs to achieve maximum distance. Pick the rocket that travels the farthest and conduct a classwide experiment. Launch this same rocket at ten-to-fifteen-degree increments from zero degrees to ninety degrees. That is, launch the rocket from a variety of angles from horizontal to vertical. Record the distance of each flight along with the angle of the launch.

In the classroom after the class finishes testing the rockets, copy the data on to the board and instruct students to make a graph with the horizontal axis representing distance and the vertical axis representing angle of launch. Have students come to you individually to show you their graph and explain the story it tells. Finally, allow students to attempt to launch their rockets over the school by picking the optimal angle (using the graph as reference) for launching.

## Variations

Suggest teams try other sizes and weights of paper.

## References

For more information on pneumatic blast rockets, see *Inventing Toys: Kids Having Fun Learning Science* (Zephyr Press, 2002).

Name: _____

# Pneumatic Blast Rocket

## CHALLENGE

Design, build, and test a pneumatic blast rocket that can be launched as far as possible.

## DESIGN

Think about what a rocket looks like and what an airplane looks like. What are the design differences? How many design differences can you think of? List them here.

_____

_____

_____

_____

_____

## INSTRUCTIONS FOR INVENTORS

Examine the fuselage your rocket scientist (teacher) shows you. Then ask yourself what you need to add to make the rocket travel a very far distance. Make one change and test launch your rocket. Record the distance it travels. Evaluate the impact of that change based on the distance the rocket flew and its flight characteristics. Then make another change and test it.

## TOY INVENTOR'S LOG

| Changes made | Distance flown |
|---|---|
| First design | |
| | |
| | |
| | |
| | |
| | |

# Pneumatic Blast Rocket

List the design changes that made the biggest improvements in your rocket's flight:

1. _____

2. _____

3. _____

4. _____

5. _____

Name: _____

# Pneumatic Blast Rocket

## TEST

Test your rocket at the angles specified below and record the distance it travels.

| Launch angle (degrees) | Distance flown (units) |
|:---:|:---:|
| 0 | |
| 10 | |
| 20 | |
| 30 | |
| 40 | |
| 50 | |
| 60 | |
| 70 | |
| 80 | |
| 90 | |

Name: _____

# Pneumatic Blast Rocket

Graph the data from the previous handout with the distance flown on the horizontal axis and the launch angle on the vertical axis.

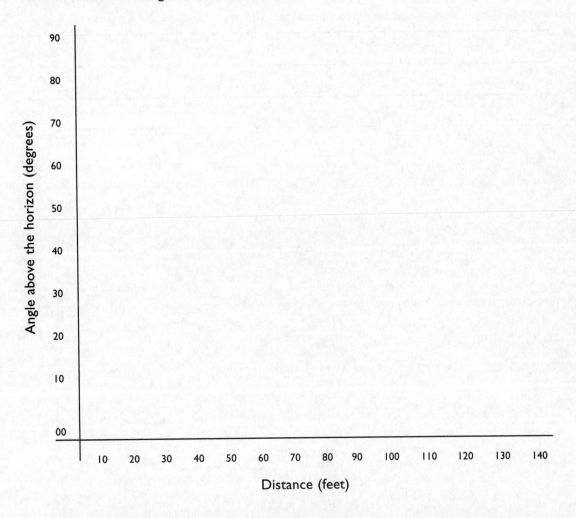

Examine the graph. What angle would you select to produce the longest launch?

## REFLECT

Science is learning through experience. To learn about scientific principles, you must be able to observe what happens and report it accurately. Once you understand what happened, you can try to determine what caused the effects you observed. You can make a hypothesis—an educated guess. Then, you can test the hypothesis in an experiment. In each experiment, change one and only one thing, so you can observe the effect of changing that one thing. During the experiment, did you change more than

# Pneumatic Blast Rocket

one variable at a time? If you did, how could you determine which of the changes you made caused the resulting change in the trajectory?

_____

_____

_____

_____

# Fling-a-Spud

## Challenge

Launch a potato across the yard or parking lot.

## Overview

This simple potato launcher sends a cylindrical piece of spud across a distance thirty feet or more.

## Materials

Spuds, 10 lbs
EMT tubing (electrical metallic tubing or conduit)
Dowel
Hacksaw
Metal file

You can buy a length of EMT tubing for a dollar at most hardware stores. To determine what size dowel to buy, take the pipe to the area of the store where wood is sold and find the largest dowel that fits inside.

## Design Concept

The dowel will push a piece of potato up the pipe. The potato forms a tight seal with the inside of the pipe, preventing air from escaping around it. A second piece of potato blocks the air from escaping out the other end. As the moving spud slides up the pipe, it compresses the air between itself and the second piece of potato. The air pressure increases until it reaches a level high enough to overcome the frictional forces holding the upper potato. It comes out the end at a high speed.

## Getting Started

Cut the EMT pipe with a hacksaw to a length one inch shorter than the dowel. Sand or file the rough edges of the pipe.

Launch the potato. To load a spud, place the "astro-potato" on top of the upright end of the EMT pipe. Pound it into the pipe with the flat of your hand. Flip the pipe over and repeat. One piece of potato will be the projectile and the other will form the seal to keep air from escaping as you fire the launcher.

Jam the dowel into one end. Insert an inch or two of the dowel into the pipe and then flip the apparatus upside down so the dowel is on the ground. To launch your "spud-nik," pull the EMT pipe down with gusto. One piece of potato will take off with a satisfying sound, and the other will dribble out the end of the tube and fall to the ground.

## Teachable Moments

Ask students why the potato flies out of the pipe. What happens inside the pipe to cause the potato piece to come out? Why does it stay in the pipe before launching? (Frictional forces keep the potato in place.) What happens if you push the dowel up slowly? (Air escapes through small openings between the potatoes and the inside walls of the pipe, so the potato doesn't fly.) Will the potato fly farther if you pull the launcher down faster? (Yes.)

## Testing

Facilitate testing by setting up a launch line and indicating the direction in which the launches should occur. Position teams as far apart as possible to prevent anyone getting hit by a flying spud bit.

Pound a cylinder of potato into each end of the metal pipe (electrical conduit). Forcing a wooden dowel inside the pipe sends one spud chunk across the yard.

# Fling-a-Spud

## CHALLENGE

Launch a piece of potato as far as possible using compressed air.

## TEST

Launch spuds several times. Each time measure and record the distance from the launch tube to the spud splat zone.

| Test number | Distance (units) |
|---|---|
| 1 | |
| 2 | |
| 3 | |
| 4 | |
| 5 | |

What factors contribute to launching a spud as far as possible?

1. _____

2. _____

3. _____

## EXTEND

Launch 2 pieces of potato at the same time. Jam 2 "spud-niks" in the end of the tube. Measure how far each travels and record the distances.

Launching 2 pieces of potato gave the following distances:

Spud #1 _____ (units) _____ Spud #2 _____ (units) _____

Compare the distance the 2 spuds traveled to the distance traveled by a single spud. If you add the 2 distances of the 2 pieces of spud, does the sum equal the distance of a single spud? Why or why not?

# Dynamic Ping-Pong Ball Launcher

## Challenge

Launch ping-pong balls across a gym.

## Overview

This device will launch ping-pong balls forty feet or more. The launcher sucks the balls out of your hand, pulls them up into a stream of air from a vacuum cleaner or shop vacuum, and flings them farther than you would imagine.

## Materials

12 ping-pong balls
PVC pipe, 1.5″ diameter
PVC "T" fitting, 1.5″ diameter
Hacksaw
Blower or vacuum cleaner with a blower

Not all vacuum cleaners let you attach the hose to the "blow" side (rather than the vacuum side), so check your vacuum before using it for this activity. A leaf blower or shop vacuum will also work well.

## Design Concept

Fast-moving air can push ping-pong balls out a tube. What's more interesting is that the same fast-moving air can suck balls up, against the force of gravity, into an airstream.

The trick to building this launcher is to position the blower nozzle so it creates low pressure on the pipe that feeds balls into a launch tube.

## Getting Started

Cut three pieces of the PVC pipe; two of the lengths are not critical to the success of the project, but one is. The barrel can be almost any length and I suggest making it two to three feet long. The feeder pipe can be about one foot long. The third pipe has to be cut precisely to fit your blower. You'll construct the launcher and then figure out how long to cut the third PVC pipe.

The feeder pipe fits into the middle opening of the "T" fitting and the barrel fits into one of the ends. You don't need to glue these, as the air pressure isn't sufficient to push them apart.

Insert the nozzle of the blower into the third leg of the "T" fitting. You want the end of the nozzle to extend so it's even with the opening of the middle leg, which is

A blower or shop vacuum provides the air stream that sucks ping-pong balls up the feed tube and out the end of the longer tube.

connected to the feeder pipe. If the nozzle extends farther than the edge of the middle opening, you'll need to add a piece of PVC pipe to space it correctly.

On the other hand, if the nozzle doesn't fit into the "T" fitting or doesn't extend far enough, you'll need to make an extension for the nozzle with some cardboard. Wrap a piece of cereal box cardboard or poster board around the end of the nozzle to form a cone that will extend to the edge of the middle leg. Tape the cone in place.

Launch the balls. You may want to tape the blower nozzle to the PVC fitting or pipe so you don't have to juggle this while you're loading balls. It's helpful to have a partner or even two to help, as you will quickly run out of hands.

With the nozzle in place, turn on the blower. Air should stream out of the barrel. Put your hand over the feeder pipe—you should feel suction. If not, you need to reposition the nozzle either farther in or farther out.

When the nozzle is positioned so you can feel suction, point the feeder down toward the floor. Point the barrel so the ball won't do any harm when it exits the tube. Hold a ball up to the feeder pipe and let it get sucked in. With a pleasant "wallop" sound the ball will travel up to the top of the "T" fitting and get spit out the end of the barrel. You can launch a dozen balls in just a few seconds.

## Teachable Moments

Challenge students to describe what is happening and why. Fast-moving air has low pressure, and this characteristic pulls air up the feeder tube. Ping-pong balls get sucked up the tube.

The same air stream that launches ping-pong balls will balance a beach ball in midair. Take the nozzle out of the launcher and aim it skyward. Hold an inflated beach ball in the stream and let the ball go. It will stay in the stream, even if you tap it on one side and even if you tilt the nozzle away from a vertical orientation.

## Variations

Students could cut several launch tubes of various lengths and test which tube produces the farthest launches. They could also try different lengths for the loading tube.

Name: _____

# Dynamic Ping-Pong Ball Launcher

## CHALLENGE

Launch a ping-pong ball as far as possible using a blower-powered launcher.

## DESIGN

Sketch the launcher illustrating where the blower connects to the pipe. Include dimensions of the launcher in your sketch. Be sure to include the units of measurement (inches, centimeters, etc.)

# Dynamic Ping-Pong Ball Launcher

## TEST

Record how far a single ball flies. Measure from the end of the launch tube to the place where the ball first hits ground. How far does a ping-pong ball fly? _____ (units) _____

## REFLECT

Where does the energy come from that launches the balls?

Why do the balls slow down?

What design features could you change to get longer launches?

## EXTEND

Experiment with different lengths of launch tube. Cut the PVC pipe into lengths that are 1 foot longer and 1 foot shorter than the tube you used initially. Test these and record the distances each launches a ball. Also indicate the overall length of the launch tube.

| Length of launch tube (units) | Distance of launch (units) |
|---|---|
|  |  |
|  |  |
|  |  |

To get an even longer launch, what length of launch tube would you recommend?

_____

If time and materials permit, test your prediction.

# Boomerang

## Challenge

Make and throw a boomerang that returns to your hand.

## Overview

Experience tells us that when we throw something it will travel away from us and not come back. What's captivating about boomerangs is that they return. Students can make simple boomerangs in a couple of hours.

## Materials

Balsa wood, ⅛″ thick sheets (full sheet or half sheet)
Rulers (1 per team)
Pens (1 per team)
Sanding blocks (1 per team)
Wood glue
Hot glue
Drill with ¼″ bit
¼″ dowel
Stopwatch

Make sanding blocks from strips of ⅜-inch plywood. Purchase a ¾-inch belt for a belt sander. Cut it into pieces about ten inches long. Glue each piece onto a strip of plywood that is as long as the belt and just a bit wider.

## Design Concept

This is a four-arm boomerang. It is made of two identical slats of balsa wood into which students sand wing shapes.

## The Details

Cut two strips of balsa wood, each one inch wide and nine inches long. If you are working

The four-arm boomerang has edges shaped into leading (L) edges and trailing (T) edges.

with younger kids, you might want to precut these with an Exacto knife. Or direct kids to cut the wood by repeatedly scoring it with a pen and rescoring it on the obverse side.

It's critical to properly mark the four edges to be sanded. In the photo, "L" denotes leading edges and "T" denotes trailing edges. So each strip of wood will have a leading edge on one side at one end and a leading edge on the other side at the opposite end.

Use sanding blocks to shape the wings or arms. The leading edge is on the right and trailing edge is on the left in the photograph. Sand the leading edge to a forty-five-degree angle. Sand the rest of the wing from about one-sixth of the distance from the leading edge back to the trailing edge.

When the wings are sanded smooth, align them so that they sit one on top of the other. Carefully drill a ¼-inch hole (you can twist the bit by hand through the soft balsa) through the center of the wings. Insert a ¼-inch dowel, mark its length, and cut it to fit so it will be flush with the top and bottom.

Each arm takes the shape of the cross section of an airplane wing. The leading edge is on the right and the trailing edge is on the left.

Use a ¼-inch drill bit to auger a hole into the soft balsa wood arms. A short piece of ¼-inch dowel glued into the hole helps hold the arms together.

Glue the dowel in place, making sure that the wings are perpendicular to each other. Also apply glue to the inside surfaces of the two wings where they will touch. Let the glue dry.

Launch the boomerang by holding it vertically in your right hand, with the flat side to the right. Face forty-five degrees to the right of any wind (if the wind is blowing strong enough to stand flags out from their poles, **don't throw**) and fling it with lots of spin. Give the boomerang lots of flick (rotation) and not much arm push (forward throw). With practice, you will throw the boomerang so it comes back.

What if your boomerang doesn't come back? If it lands to your left, throw it farther to the right. If it lands in front of you, aim higher. If it runs out of steam and doesn't return, add some weight (such as drops of hot glue or paper clips attached to the ends of the arms). If it lands behind you, try using less "arm."

Why do boomerangs return? A tendency to spin and an asymmetric shape are essential properties of a boomerang. The thrower holds the boomerang vertically by one end and spins it as he or she throws it. The wing shaped surface of each arm creates lift. Lift on the upper arm is greater since it is spinning in the same direction the boomerang is traveling. Lift on the lower arm is less since it's moving in the opposite direction the boomerang is traveling. The air speed measured on the upper arm is the combination of the boomerang's forward motion plus the forward spin of the upper arm. On the lower arm, the measured air speed is forward speed minus the speed of rotation. The speed of air over the wing determines lift.

Since the boomerang flies vertically, an increased lift on the upper arm causes the top of the boomerang to lean to the left side. However, the boomerang spins and the lift-generated torque causes the boomerang to turn to the left. (If you lean to the left when riding a bicycle, you put torque on the front wheel. But instead of falling to the left, the wheel turns to the left. Try leaning to one side when the bicycle wheels aren't spinning and you'll go "kersplat" on the ground.)

The left turn is the first part of the boomerang's trajectory. As it turns, the boomerang lays over so it's nearly horizontal and the force of lift causes it to rise. After reaching the top of its trajectory, now about half way around the circle, the boomerang falls back to the thrower.

**Don't try to catch these with one hand. Catch a boomerang by putting one hand in the air and the other hand beneath the boomerang and bringing your hands together to snag it.**

Lefties need not be left out. They can throw a boomerang made for right-handed throwers following the same directions that righties use as they throw, but lefties throw with their left hands. This gives the boomerang a counterclockwise flight, the same as for righties. Reverse the leading and trailing edges of a boomerang to make it a lefty boomerang. To fling the lefty boomerang, reverse the directions given above and the boomerang will travel in a clockwise path.

## Teachable Moments

Boomerangs are counterintutitive and difficult to understand. Inspire students to feel a sense of awe that something they throw can come back and that the universe is filled with cool stuff to marvel at and try to understand.

## Variations

This design is robust enough to work with other lengths, widths, and thicknesses of wood. Students could use the same design to make other boomerangs and compare their flight characteristics to the original. They could measure the diameter of the path and compare it to the length and weight of each boomerang.

Name: _____

# Boomerang

## CHALLENGE

Make a wooden boomerang that returns to you after you've thrown it.

## DESIGN

This boomerang consists of two identical wings that are joined at their centers to form an "X." The shape of the wings is critical. Examine the shape of the wings of the boomerang your teacher made. You will see the shape looks like an airplane wing when viewed from the end of one wing. As you rotate the boomerang around its center and view the other three wings, you will see that each one has the same shape. The end of each wing is shaped like an airplane wing, while the center of each looks less like a wing.

Looking at one wing from the top, you see that unlike an airplane wing, the leading edge (steep edge) is on oppostive sides of opposite ends.

Before starting to shape the wings, make sure you know which side of each wing you should shape into leading edges and which you should shape into trailing edges.

## INSTRUCTIONS FOR INVENTORS

Follow your teacher's guidance in building the boomerang.

## TEST

Once your boomerang works and will return close to your throwing location (**don't try to catch the boomerang as the fast-spinning arms will hurt**), time its flight with a stopwatch.

Make at least 3 measurements and average them.

| Test flight # | Time (seconds) |
|---|---|
| 1 | |
| 2 | |
| 3 | |
| Average time | |

To get the average time, add the times from the test flights and divide that number by the number of test flights.

Add weights to the arms of your boomerang and retest its flight time. With hot glue, secure 1 or more large paper clips to the ends of each arm of the boomerang and then measure the boomerang's time aloft. How does adding weight change the time?

_____

# Pressure Rocket Launcher

## Challenge

Design, build, and test a rocket that uses a bicycle pump as an energy source.

## Overview

This launcher uses the same conceptual design as popular toys, but you can make it for under $5, not counting the cost of a bicycle pump. The bike pump must have a pressure gauge, and you need to exercise responsibility and be aware of safety issues.

Have students charge the launcher with a bike pump so they can measure the pressure and compare it to the distance their rockets fly. Having them work the pump gives them an intuitive feel for the work required to launch a rocket.

## Materials

Launcher:
  PVC pipe, schedule 40, 1″ diameter
  PVC ball valve, 1″ diameter
  PVC end cap, 1″ diameter
  PVC cleaner and cement
  Saw that will cut PVC pipe
  Tire stem from a bicycle inner tube
  Hot glue
  Drill and bits
  Pliers
  Bike pump (that stands on the floor) with pressure gauge
Rockets:
  Scrap office paper
  Paper clips
  Masking tape
  Scissors
  Eye goggles
  Index cards

The PVC pipe is inexpensive, so purchase a length of eight or ten feet, whichever length is easily transportable. Almost any saw (wood, coping, or hack) will cut the pipe.

You can find tire stems at bike stores. Ask the staff for inner tubes they are going to throw away, and cut out the valve stem.

## Design Concept

The launcher consists of two tubes separated by a ball valve. One tube is closed at the end and the bike tire valve protrudes from it. With a bike pump you increase the pressure inside this end tube. The rocket slides onto the open-ended tube. Opening the valve releases the pressure required to launch the rocket.

## The Details

To make the launcher, drill a ⁵⁄₁₆-inch hole in the center of the end cap to accommodate the valve stem from the bike inner tube. Cut the valve stem out of the inner tube, leaving a ring of rubber around its base that you will use to secure the valve. Plastics glue works well to attach the valve to the ring of rubber, but hot glue works better. Smear the glue liberally around the base of the tire stem. Jam it through the hole in the end cap from inside, so the inflating opening will be outside the launcher. Grab hold of the stem with pliers and pull tightly until the glue sets (this is why fast-setting hot glue is preferable). Be careful not to whack the tire stem as it is easy to dislodge and difficult to reseal.

Cut three lengths of pipe about eighteen inches long. Clean the burrs off the cut ends and glue two of them to the ball valve, following the instructions on the PVC cleaner and glue. Glue the end cap with tire valve protruding to one of the pipe ends. Set the launcher aside to allow the cement to cure, following the directions on the PVC cement container.

To make a rocket, wrap a piece of paper around the third piece of pipe that you cut. Make sure the paper fits loosely enough that it will slide off and on the pipe. Tape the edge to hold the paper together in a tube.

Hold one end of the paper tube between the thumbs and middle fingers of both your hands. In this position use your index fingers to push the open end nearly closed. Just before the paper touches, collapse the end of the tube between your thumbs and middle fingers. Tape this shut.

Here is a rocket ready to launch.

To make the end airtight, fold it over and tape it again. Test the rocket by blowing into the open end of the pipe and listening for air escaping from the other end.

Add two or three paper clips to the tape end and wrap them with a layer of masking tape to hold them in place. Otherwise the paper clips tend to fly off during every launch.

Students should experiment to figure out that they need to add fins and a nose cone. Index cards make good fins and cones.

Launch the rocket. **Use discretion when launching a rocket and wear eye protection.** Turn the handle of the ball valve to close it. The handle should be perpendicular to the pipe. Connect the bike pump to the tire stem and pump. Listen for leaks where the stem emerges from the end cap and where the pipe attaches to the ball valve. A slight leak at the tire stem may not present a problem, as increasing air pressure will tend to seal it.

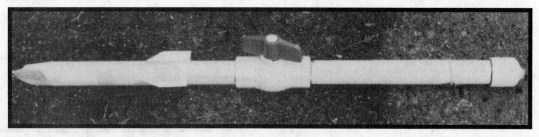

A pressure rocket is on the launch tube. The ball valve in the middle keeps air in the reservoir until ready to launch. The tire stem valve connects to a bike pump.

Slide a rocket onto the end of the launcher. Be careful not to catch the inner edge of paper on the launcher. Pointing the rocket in a safe direction, turn the handle of the ball valve as quickly as possible.

These rockets will fly vertically at least five or six stories. If yours does not fly that high, watch the rocket closely. A wobbly trajectory suggests that either the fins aren't effective or the nose cone isn't symmetric. Ensure that the fins are aligned parallel to each other and attached solidly at the base of the rocket. Check out the nose; is it smashed to one side? After a few crash landings, nose cones can get bent out of joint and will need repair or replacement.

## Getting Started

Ask students to think of all the devices people use that require air or fluid pressure to work. They may think of a bike or ball pump and possibly scuba equipment. Other suggestions include pneumatic tires, balloons, mechanics wrenches, hydraulic lifts and jacks, and hydraulic elevators. In this experiment they release air pressure suddenly to accelerate rockets.

## Teachable Moments

While a student is laboring at the pump, ask him or her where the energy comes from to launch a rocket. Pursue this line of questioning back to the ultimate source of energy for this planet, the sun.

After each launch ask teams what their rocket did. If they are able to answer correctly, ask them why the rocket performed as they described. They should be able to point to a feature of their rocket responsible for its trajectory. Then ask them what single change they could make to improve their rocket. Repeat this line of questioning at each launch and students will learn to be ready with responses.

Name: _____

# Pressure Rocket Launcher

## CHALLENGE

Make a rocket powered by a bicycle pump that flies as far as possible.

## DESIGN

Draw a picture of a rocket, illustrating the features that help it fly.

# Pressure Rocket Launcher

## INSTRUCTIONS FOR INVENTORS

1.  Construct a rocket that follows the design you drew. Use a sheet of paper for the fuselage (body of the rocket). To make sure the rocket fits onto the launcher, use a piece of the PVC pipe as a mold.
2.  Wrap the paper around the pipe. Make sure the edge is straight (parallel to the fuselage). Loosen the paper so the pipe slides easily through it and then tape the paper along the seam.

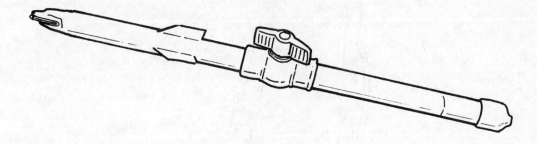

A pressure rocket is on the launch tube. The ball valve in the middle keeps air in the reservoir until the rocket is ready to be launched. The tire stem valve connects to a bike pump.

3.  Seal one end. Hold one end of the paper tube between the thumbs and middle fingers of both your hands. In this position use your index fingers to push the open end nearly closed. Just before the paper touches, collapse the end of the tube between thumbs and middle fingers. Tape this shut.
4.  To make the end airtight, fold it over and tape it again. Test by blowing into the open end of the pipe and listening for air escaping from the other end.

Name: _____

# Pressure Rocket Launcher

Use available materials (paper, index cards, paper clips, and masking tape) to complete your rocket.

Ask the launcher master (your teacher) to approve your rocket before testing it.

## TEST

**Everyone should wear safety goggles.** Pump the bike pump (connected to the launcher) to a pressure of 30 pounds per square inch. Slide the rocket onto the end of the launcher. The launcher master will launch it for you.

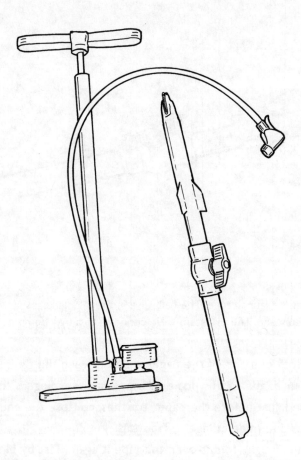

A pressure rocket launcher with bike pump. Connect the pump to the inflating valve, and pump, with the launcher handle closed. To launch a rocket, insert it on the open end of the launcher and open the handle.

If your rocket flies in a straight line, measure the distance it traveled. If it doesn't fly in a straight line, make changes to the rocket's design so it will fly straight.

Name: _____

# Pressure Rocket Launcher

Improve your rocket and test it, recording the distance it traveled each time and what improvement you made. Include the units of measurement. Use 30 psi for each launch.

## TOY INVENTOR'S LOG

| Launch number | Changes made | Distance (units) |
|---|---|---|
| 1 | Initial rocket | |
| 2 | | |
| 3 | | |
| 4 | | |
| 5 | | |
| 6 | | |
| 7 | | |

Use your best rocket design to test how far a rocket will travel at different pressures. Launch the rocket without making changes to it (unless you need to fix a broken part) and measure the distance it travels (range).

| Launch number | Pressure (psi) | Range (units) |
|---|---|---|
| | 130 | |
| | 240 | |
| | 350 | |
| | 460 | |
| | 570 | |

psi = pounds of pressure per square inch.

What is the relationship between pressure and range? As pressure increases, what happens to range?

_____

Name: _____

# Pressure Rocket Launcher

Where did the energy that propelled the rocket come from?

_____

Between launches, feel the outside of the pump. Is it warm?

_____

Why might you expect the pump to be warm?

_____

Name: _____

# Pressure Rocket Launcher

In the time remaining make improvements to your rocket to get it to fly as far as possible. Try to establish a school record for rocket launches. Record the changes you make after each launch and the distance your rocket flies at 60 psi.

| Changes we made to the rocket | Range (units) at 60 psi |
|---|---|
| | |
| | |
| | |
| | |
| | |
| | |
| | |
| | |
| | |
| | |
| | |
| | |

Design improvements:

1. If your rocket doesn't fly very far, trim the fins so they provide less air resistance. You'll know you've cut too far when your rocket flies erratically.

2. Add weight to the nose. Add 1 or 2 large paper clips to the nose and tape them in place. If this improves the range, try adding more. If adding more decreases the range, take some off.

Name: _____

# Pressure Rocket Launcher

3. Improve the symmetry of the nose cone so that it has the same shape on all sides, like an ice cream cone.

## EXTEND

This project has several other fun science activities embedded in it. A comparison of a rocket's length of travel (range) to its launch pressure would make a great graph. Investigate the length of travel for different fin designs or fin surface areas. Construct a device to measure the angle of launch and compare it to the flight distance. Since weight (number of paper clips) makes significant contributions to the range, you could measure and compare these numbers. You could also try different barrel lengths and different amounts of pressure on the launcher to see how they impact flight.

# Chemical Minirocket

## Challenge

Build a rocket powered by a chemical reaction.

## Overview

This rocket will launch six or seven feet in the air, powered by the carbon dioxide released by one antacid tablet.

## Materials

Empty translucent 35 mm film canisters (1 per team)
Alka-Seltzer tablets or generic antacid tablets (6 per team)
Water
Teaspoon
Stopwatch (1 per team)

## Design Concepts

A quick chemical reaction (combine water and tablet) generates carbon dioxide gas. The gas takes up much more volume than the solid and liquid components. As the reaction continues to generate gas, the pressure increases until it exceeds the frictional forces holding the lid on the canister.

This same concept is used by the safety air bags in cars. On impact, a chemical reaction is initiated that releases nitrogen in a fraction of a second. (See http://www.howstuffworks.com/airbag.htm for an explanation.) The gas fills the air bag to protect you in a collision.

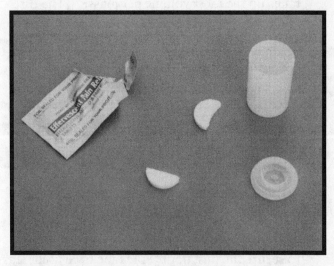

The chemical rocket uses a piece of an antacid tablet and some water in a clear film canister to produce a chemical reaction.

## The Details

Fill a clear film canister half way with water. Break tablets in half and drop one half into the canister. Quickly snap on the lid and place the canister, lid down, on a counter. **Don't put it on the floor where it could launch into someone's eye.**

This project can get messy, so plan for water and partially dissolved tablets to be spilled wherever you launch these rockets.

## Getting Started

Ask students which state of matter (solid, liquid, or gas) takes up the most room per weight. They should know that solids and liquids fall to the ground if dropped; that is, they have a higher weight per volume or higher density than gas. Some solids float on water, and some sink. So, in general, which state of matter takes up the most volume of space for a given weight? Demonstrate how a rocket works by launching a few.

## Teachable Moments

After observing several launches, students should be able to describe what is happening when the rocket lifts off. Prompt them along with questions. "What causes the rocket to blast off?" (The carbon dioxide gas released in the chemical reaction powers the rocket.) "Where did the gas come from?" (It is the product of the chemical reaction between the tablet and water.) "What are the three states of matter and which takes up the most volume per mass?" (The three states of matter are solid [the tablet], liquid [water], and gas [carbon dioxide]. Gas takes up much more volume per unit of mass.) "Why is this called a chemical reaction?" (In chemical reactions, materials are changed. The tablet dissolves, releasing gas.)

## Testing

Students will test the duration of launches with different quantities of water in the film canisters. They will have to split the tablets approximately in half and use one half for each experiment.

## Variations

Add fins to the rocket to test if the fins improve the launch height. Use masking tape to secure the fins, double the tape over itself, leaving a small piece at each end to stick to the canister. You could also measure the "throw weight" that this rocket has. Add paper clips until the weight of the rocket exceeds the force available for liftoff.

You can experiment with other propellants like baking soda and vinegar, but we've found nothing that works as well as an Alka-Seltzer tablet. A full tablet doesn't produce any better results than a half tablet.

Name: _____

# Chemical Minirocket

## CHALLENGE

Use the chemical reaction produced by adding water to an antacid tablet to launch a rocket. Test your rocket to find the optimal amount of water you should add to make the rocket fly as high as possible.

## TEST

Time the rocket's flight to see what quantity of water produces the longest flight time. Use a half teaspoon to measure water. If time and materials permit, repeat the experiment and increase the amount of water by ½-teaspoon increments. If not, repeat the experiment for increments of 1 teaspoon. Use a ½ tablet of antacid for each experiment.

| Number of half teaspoons of water | Duration of launch (units) |
|:---:|:---:|
| 1 | |
| 2 | |
| 3 | |
| 4 | |
| 5 | |
| 6 | |
| 7 | |
| 8 | |
| 9 | |
| 10 | |

Use graph paper to display the data. What is the optimal quantity of water you used to get the longest flight time?

_____

# On the Water

Boats are as much fun to design, construct, and test as cars and planes, maybe even more fun. However, they require facilities for launching. Weather and safety also constrain when and where your students can test their boats. However, on a warm spring or summer day, experimenting with boats can be great fun and provide opportunities for learning. You can make a simple test tank if your school or museum isn't blessed with suitable fountains or ponds.

To integrate these hands-on projects with written assignments, have students research any of the following inventors or inventions and connect their explorations to the toy research embedded in the activities below.

David Bushnell, designer of the *Turtle*, one of the first submarines
John Ericsson, inventor of the ship's screw and designer of the *USS Monitor*
Ole Evinrude, inventor of the outboard motor
John Fitch, American inventor of the steamship
Robert Fulton, owner of the *Clermont*, the first commercially successful steamship
*Savannah*, the first nuclear-powered merchant ship
Elmer Sperry, inventor of the ship's gyroscopic compass
Ericsson and Sperry are in the National Inventors
      Hall of Fame (http://www.invent.org).

A school fountain or kids' wading pool can work well as a testing basin. Basins you build will work even better for this activity. Two different designs are outlined below.

## Materials

ABS (or PVC) sewer pipe, 6" diameter and 13′ long
Jigsaw
4 endcaps for pipe, or 3 1″ × 4″ 8′ boards
Saw
Screws and driver or nails and hammer
Plastic tarp (at least 5′ × 10′)

To make a basin for boats to travel in a straight line, use a long water-filled section of six-inch diameter plastic pipe. This is called sewer pipe in hardware stores. To make a test trough, cut a long (twelve-foot) PVC pipe in half lengthwise. This cut makes two troughs that allow teams to race each other. Purchase four end caps for the pipes or make end caps by cutting semicircles traced from the inside of the pipe out of wood. Glue and screw the semicircles in place. You could put small wedges under the pipe to help hold the pipe in position, but once the pipe is filled with water it is fairly stable.

To make a larger test basin, purchase three pine boards (eleven by eight feet) and cut one in half. The eight-foot boards form the two long sides of the basin and the four-foot sections form the ends.

Nail or screw the boards together so they can stand on edge. To make the basin easy to store, connect the boards with hinges that have removable pins.

Once the four-foot by eight-foot basin is laid out, cover it with a large sheet of ten mil plastic sheeting or more durable plastic tarp. Fill the basin with a hose. As the water flows in to the basin, it will pull the plastic into place.

Here are two easy ways to make test tanks. On the right is a thirteen-foot long, six-inch diameter PVC pipe cut in half lengthwise. On the left are three pine boards held together with nuts and bolts. A vinyl sheet drapes inside the wood frame and keeps the water in the basin.

# Gravity-Powered Boat

## Challenge

Construct a boat powered by gravity that travels as far as possible in a straight line.

## Overview

The idea of making a boat propelled by the force of gravity can boggle the mind. This activity provides a simple way of making a gravity-powered boat. Use this project either as a quick activity to demonstrate the applications of gravity or as an extended activity that challenges students to engineer solutions to several problems.

## Materials

Straws (various diameters)
Bendable straws (various diameters)
Plastic or styrene disposable dinner plates
Styrofoam cup (1 per team, plus spares)
Duct tape
Hot glue
Nail or awl

## Design Concept

Water flowing out of a Styrofoam cup provides the propulsion for this boat.

## The Details

The hull is made of two disposable dinner plates glued edge to edge. The motor is held in a cup, glued to the center of the top plate. Poke a hole with a nail or an awl into the base of the cup and insert a straw. You want the straw to fit snugly.

Launch the boat in a still pond or wading pool. You don't need the water to be more than two to three feet deep. Scoop a cup of water from the basin with

Water flowing out of the cup drives the gravity-powered boat.

a second cup and pour the water into the motor. The boat will begin to move immediately.

## Getting Started

Students could labor a long time before figuring out how to make the basic model, so you should show them how a gravity-powered boat works. Then student teams can innovate the basic design to make their boats travel farther in a straight line.

## Teachable Moments

As the boats are moving across the water ask students, "In what direction is the water flowing out of the straw?" Have them point to show you the direction. Then ask, "What direction is the boat going in?" Point out that the water is moving in the direction opposite to the boat. Draw parallels with bicycles, walking, and skating: in each case, you push backward to move forward.

## Variations

Use duct tape to cover holes in the cup or to make holes of different sizes. After trying one size hole, students can cover the hole with duct tape and make a new hole to try other size straws.

Name: _____

# Gravity-Powered Boat

## CHALLENGE

Make and test a boat powered by the force of gravity.

## DESIGN

Your fleet commander (teacher) will show you a working model of a gravity-powered boat. Then you can make your own model and improve it so that it travels as far as possible.

Water flowing out of the cup drives the gravity-powered boat.

## TEST

When your boat is working, address the following questions by conducting experiments with your boat.

What happens if you point the straw off to one side? The boat moves

_____.

How far can you get the boat to travel in a straight line?

_____ (units) _____

What could you do to make it travel farther? _____
Test your idea.

Would the boat go farther if you used a larger straw or a smaller straw?

_____

Name: _____

## Gravity-Powered Boat

How could you test your idea?

_____

Do it!

Could you connect 2 straws instead of just 1? What happens?

_____

How far did the boat go with 2 straws?

_____

Can you make a boat with two gravity engines? Try it. Did it go twice as far?

_____

Why or why not?

_____

Can you make your boat turn in a tight circle? How did you do it? _____

_____

## REFLECT

What propelled the boat?

_____

What physical constraints limit how big you could make a gravity boat?

_____

# Electric Boat

## Challenge

Make a boat powered by a battery that travels as far and as fast as possible.

## Overview

This boat zips across the water and is powered by an inexpensive electric motor and battery. This activity provides a hands-on introduction to electricity and direct current circuits, as well as motion and forces.

## Materials

> Quart or half-gallon paper milk or juice containers
>> (at least 1 for every 2 teams)
>
> Scissors (1 pair per team)
>
> Direct current motors (1 per team)
>
> Alligator clip leads (2 per team, plus spares)
>
> D batteries (1 per team, plus spares)
>
> Battery holders (1 per team)
>
> Cocktail straws (1 per team, plus spares)
>
> Hot glue
>
> Rubber bands (1 bag)
>
> Aluminum foil
>
> Duct tape
>
> Awl or sharp nail
>
> Testing basin

If you cannot find battery holders, direct students to use rubber bands to hold the wires or clip leads to the battery terminals.

## Design Concept

Students make propellers out of aluminum foil and attach them to propeller shafts (cocktail straws) that fit onto the shafts of direct current motors.

## Getting Started

If students aren't familiar with electric motors, allow them to examine the motors and batteries for a few minutes. Give each team two clip

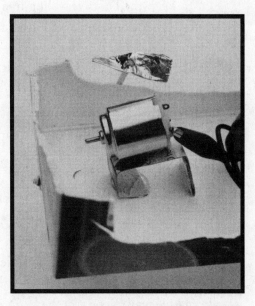

The motor for the electric boat is attached to a motor mount to get the optimal angle for the shaft and propeller.

leads, one battery, and one motor. Ask them to check the motors to make sure that they work (the students will figure out how to transfer electrical power to the motors). Ask them to observe which direction the motor spins and then challenge them to make the motor spin in the opposite direction.

## Teachable Moments

As students test their boats, you will have opportunities to add to their learning experience. When teams first get their motors to spin, ask them how they connected the battery to the motor. Point out that a circuit needs to be "complete" to work. That is, one wire must connect one side of a battery to one terminal of a motor and a second wire must connect the other side of the battery to the other motor terminal.

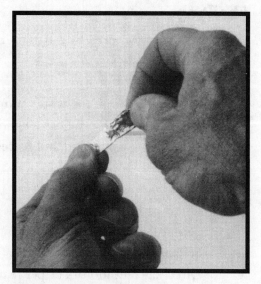

The propeller for the electric boat can be made out of a piece of aluminum foil. Once attached to the driveshaft, the ends are folded in opposite directions to give the propeller its "pitch."

Reversing either the pitch of the propeller or the polarity of the electrical connection (switching the wires connected to the battery's positive and negative terminals) will change the direction of motion.

To keep the boats traveling in a straight line, suggest that teams add a rudder or keel. Or they could reposition the motor to eliminate the turning.

## Testing

The challenge is to make an electric boat with an in-water propeller that can travel the length of the test tank. Getting the boats to move in a straight line is a difficult engineering task, so reaching the far end is quite an accomplishment.

## Variations

To make the motor spin faster, teams can add a second D battery. Most students will connect the batteries in series: the positive end of one battery will be connected to the negative end of the second battery, and the motor will connect to the alternate ends of each battery. Connecting batteries in series increases the voltage to the sum of the two batteries: in this case three volts. The motors should spin faster. Point out the alternative way to connect the batteries is to connect the two positive terminals together (and to one motor terminal) and the two negative terminals together (and to the other motor terminal). In this case, the voltage and motor speed will equal the voltage and motor speed of a single battery. However, the batteries will last twice as long in this "parallel" circuit.

If you have enough motors, allow students to add a second motor once their one-motor boat works. Direct them to test two motors, both powered by one battery, and then allow them to add a second battery.

# Electric Boat

## CHALLENGE

Build and test a boat powered by an electric motor.

## DESIGN

Imagine a power boat with an on-board motor turning a propeller that's in the water. A long propeller shaft connects the motor shaft to the propeller. Instead of using a gasoline or diesel engine, you'll use an electric motor.  Consider the following questions:

How will you connect the motor to the battery?

How will you connect the motor to the propeller?

How will you make a propeller?

How will you get the boat to travel in a straight line?

## INSTRUCTIONS FOR INVENTORS

1. Make a hull out of a milk or juice carton. Cut the carton in half lengthwise to make 2 hulls.

2. With an awl or other sharp tool poke a hole for the propeller shaft in the stern (rear of the boat) near the bottom of the carton.

3. Check to see how a small straw fits onto the shaft of the electric motor. Most likely it will slide on and off too easily. To hold the straw on the shaft, wrap the shaft 1 or more times with masking tape. Then push the small straw onto the shaft.

4. Slide the end of the propeller shaft through the opening in the hull so you can determine where to affix the motor and battery. The shaft will need to be set at a downward angle so the propeller will be fully immersed in the water.

5. Drop a glob of hot glue along the centerline of the boat and press the battery holder on top.

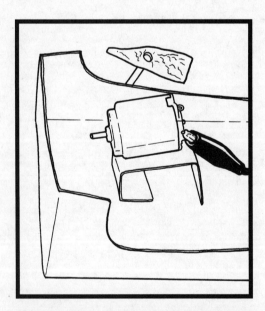

The motor on the electric boat is attached to a motor mount to get the optimal angle for the shaft and propeller.

# Electric Boat

6. Make a motor mount out of milk carton material. You need to elevate the motor so the shaft is in the correct position, exiting the hole in the boat so the propeller is in the water. Fold pieces of the carton on to themselves and glue them in place. Glue the mount to the bottom of the boat. Put another small glob of glue on the top of the mount to attach the motor so it will connect to the propeller shaft. Set the motor at an angle so propeller shaft and motor shaft are in a straight line.

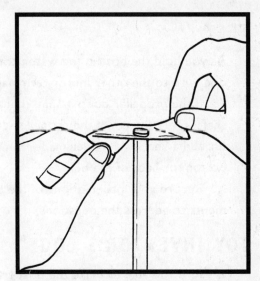

The propeller for the electric boat is made out of a piece of aluminum foil. Once attached to the driveshaft, the ends are folded in opposite directions to give the propeller its "pitch."

7. To make a propeller cut a piece of aluminum foil about 2 by 3 inches. Fold each side in half twice so the piece is about ½ by ¾ inches. With the awl, poke a hole in the center, being careful not to rip the foil. Slide the motor shaft through the propeller hole and put a drop of hot glue on each side of the propeller to hold it on to the shaft. Twist each end of the propeller in the opposite direction to give the propeller its pitch.

8. Connect one end of each alligator clip lead to the opposite terminals of the battery holder. If you don't have holders for the batteries, hold the clip leads in place by stretching a rubber band over the battery and clip leads. Connect the free end of one of the leads to a motor terminal. You're ready to test. **Do not connect a wire to both ends of a battery. This will ruin the battery.**

# Electric Boat

## TEST

As you hold the boat in the water, complete the electric circuit by connecting the second wire to the other motor terminal.

If the propeller doesn't spin, check the connections of the wires and make sure the shaft is free to turn. If the propeller drives the boat to one side, reposition the motor. Or add a keel or a rudder made from a piece of the milk carton that you glue to the bottom or back of the boat.

Record your observations of the boat on the following sheet and conduct experiments to address the questions.

## TOY INVENTOR'S LOG

1. Were you able to make the boat travel in a straight line? _____ How did you do this? _____

2. What happens if you reverse the wire leads to the motor?

   _____


3. Could you increase the motor speed by adding a second battery? Sketch a diagram showing how you would connect 2 batteries to the motor.

# Electric Boat

4.  Get a second battery and another clip lead and hook up both batteries. What happens?

    _____

5.  What happens if you reverse the pitch of the propeller? Untwist each blade of the propeller and twist them in the opposite direction. What happens when you test the boat?

    _____

6.  What could you change about the propeller to make the boat go faster? Record your ideas and test them, jotting notes so you can remember how each innovation worked.

| Idea for propeller design to improve speed | What was the observed impact of this change? |
|---|---|
| | |
| | |
| | |
| | |

7.  How else could you increase the speed of the boat? Write your ideas here and, with your teacher's permission, test them and record the results.

| Idea for improving the speed | What was the observed impact of this change? |
|---|---|
| | |
| | |
| | |

# Swamp Boat

## Challenge

Make a boat that propels itself with blowing air.

## Overview

Boats used in Florida's Everglades are pushed with airplane propellers turned by gasoline engines. Electric motors replace the gasoline engines in this activity. Concepts embedded in this activity include direct current circuits, motion, forces, and velocity.

## Materials

> Quart or half-gallon paper milk or juice containers
>     (1 for every 2 teams)
> Scissors (1 pair per team)
> Direct current motors (1 per team)
> Alligator clip leads (2 per team, plus spares)
> 9 V batteries (1 per team, plus spares)
> Airplane propellers (1 per team)
> Hot glue
> Small plastic cups or pieces of cardboard
> Testing basin
> Measuring sticks (1 for every 2 teams)
> Stopwatches (1 per team)

Propellers about 2.5 inches wide work well. When purchasing propellers, make sure that the center hole is the same size as the motor shaft diameter. Kelvin sells plastic propellers that fit on to the motor shafts of the motors they sell.

A school fountain or kids' wading pool can work for the testing basin. If you do not have access to these resources, make a small test basin using the instructions on page 165.

## Design Concept

Students attach propellers to motors and make complete circuits to operate the motors. They engineer (design and build) motor mounts with plastic cups or scrap cardboard to raise the propeller so it doesn't hit the boat or water.

## Getting Started

If students aren't familiar with electric motors, allow them to examine the motors and batteries for a few minutes. Give each team two clip leads, a propeller, a battery, and one motor. Warn them that spinning propellers will hurt if they hit fingers.

Ask them to check the motors to make sure that they work (the students will figure out how to transfer electrical power to the motors). Challenge them to reverse the direction the motor spins (by reversing the leads to the battery).

## Teachable Moments

As teams connect the motors to the batteries, ask the students questions about circuits and what makes them complete. Ask them how many different ways they could make a boat reverse its direction of travel. Also ask how they could get the boat to travel in a circle and suggest that they try.

## Testing

Teams measure the speed of their boats as they race across the length of the test tank.

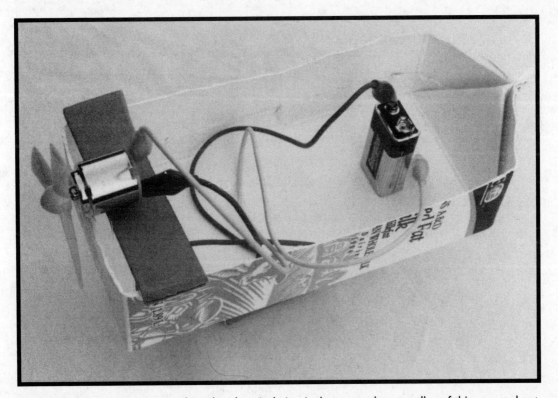

Clip leads make it easy to complete the electrical circuit that turns the propeller of this swamp boat.

## Variations

Extend this activity by suggesting that teams use a second motor and propeller. You could limit them to one battery or allow them to use a second one. Instruct them to compare the boat's speed using two motors with one battery and with two batteries.

Provide several batteries (AA or C) that teams can test. They could measure the speed of the boat powered by 1.5 volts (one battery) and multiples of 1.5 volts. To make this easier, provide as many battery holders as combinations of batteries as you can find. This experiment begs teams to summarize their results in a graph showing boat speed as a function of voltage.

# Swamp Boat

## CHALLENGE

Build and test a boat that uses a model airplane propeller.

## DESIGN

Have you seen a swamp boat? They are used in the Everglades in Florida. A swamp boat is a shallow draft boat (the hull sits high in the water) that is powered by an airplane propeller driven by a gasoline engine. You can make a model using an electric motor instead of a gasoline engine.

## INSTRUCTIONS FOR INVENTORS

1.  Make a hull from a milk or juice carton. Cut the carton in half lengthwise down the middle. Now you have 2 hulls.
2.  Figure out where you will place the motor and battery, and how you will connect the 2 together. Use a small drop of hot glue to hold the battery and motor in place. If you use more than a small drop, you will have a harder time trying to remove them. **Do not connect a wire to both ends of a battery. This will ruin the battery.**

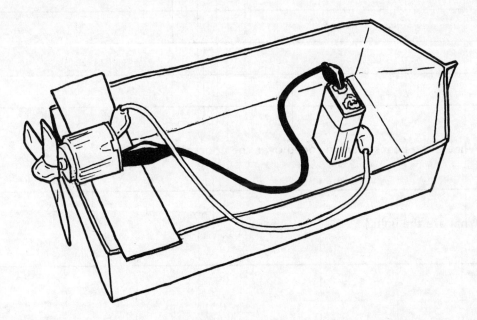

Clip leads make it easy to complete the electrical circuit that turns the propeller of this swamp boat.

# Swamp Boat

## TEST

As you hold the boat in the water, complete the electric circuit by connecting the clip leads to the motor terminals and battery terminals. Adjust the position of the motor or add skegs (fins) to make the boat travel in a straight line.

Record your observations of the boat below and conduct experiments to address the questions.

## TOY INVENTOR'S LOG

Establish a measured test course in the basin that will allow you to conduct time measurements. Record the length of the measured test course here:

_____ (units) _____

Measure the time it takes your boat to move through the measured course. Repeat the measurement twice and average the times.

| Experiment # | Elapsed time (seconds) |
|---|---|
| 1 | |
| 2 | |
| 3 | |
| Average | |

What is the boat's average speed over the course?

_____

What are the units?

_____

Name: _____

# Swamp Boat

What could you do to improve the boat's speed?

1. _____

2. _____

3. _____

Pick one of these modifications and, with your teacher's approval, implement it. Then repeat the measurements of time and compute the new speed. Record that here.

| Experiment # | Elapsed time (seconds) |
|:---:|:---:|
| 1 | |
| 2 | |
| 3 | |
| Average | |

What is the boat's average speed over the course? _____

Did the modifications to the boat improve its speed? _____

Why or why not? _____

If time permits, try another modification and determine how the change will improve the boat's speed.

# Rubber Band-Powered Boat

## Challenge

Make a boat that is powered by a single rubber band and travels as far as possible in a straight line.

## Overview

There are several ways to propel a boat with a rubber band. Two models are suggested in this activity: stern-wheelers and side-wheelers. The choice can be predicated on the width of the test tank or basin, as side-wheelers require more room. As a reward for good work, allow teams to experiment with two or more rubber bands.

## Materials

Quart and half-gallon paper milk or juice containers
(1 for every 2 teams)
Rubber bands (1 bag)
¼″ dowels, (about 20″ per team)
Scissors (1 pair per team)
Duct tape
Hot glue
Test tank or basin

## Design Concept

Paddles made of milk carton pieces are spun by a rubber band to drive the boat.

## The Details

There are several ways to power a boat with rubber bands. Most teams will extend two dowels behind the boat. Duct tape holds the dowels in place along either side of the boat. Students hang a propeller from the ends of the dowels with a rubber band. This is a stern (or bow) wheeler.

An alternative design is a side-wheeler. Teams poke holes on opposite sides of the hull to hold a dowel. They cut propellers from a milk carton and attach them to the two ends, and wrap a rubber band around the dowel to turn it. The other end of the rubber band is held in place in the transom (stern) by poking a hole in the transom and tying the band to a short piece of dowel (toggle).

## Getting Started

Younger students may need to see a model of how a rubber band–powered boat works. Many students won't be able to visualize how to make a propeller until they see one, so you could draw a diagram or show an example.

## Teachable Moments

Many students will wind their propellers in the wrong direction. After students discover their mistakes, help them verbalize what they need to do to fix the problem: wind the propeller so it unwinds, pushing water backward to move the boat forward.

## Testing

The challenge is to get boats to travel the length of the test tank.

# Rubber Band-Powered Boat

## CHALLENGE

Build a boat powered by a rubber band that can propel itself across the length of the test trough.

## DESIGN

There are 3 components of the rubber band–powered boat: the boat hull, the propeller, and the drive system. Team members can each work on 1 component.

## INSTRUCTIONS FOR INVENTORS

1. Boat hull: Use scissors to cut a paper milk or juice carton in half lengthwise. You can make either a flat-bottomed boat (by cutting along the middle of the side panels) or a "V" hull (by cutting along the edge between side panels).

2. Propeller: Use scrap milk cartons. Cut 2 pieces, each about 2 inches by 2 inches. In the center of each, cut a narrow notch halfway across. Slide the 2 pieces onto each other by aligning the 2 notches and forcing them together. Use small pieces of duct tape to hold the propeller blades 90 degrees apart.

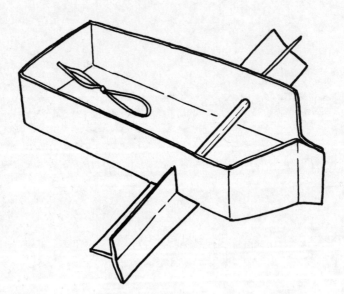

Here is a side-wheel version of the rubber band–powered boat.

# Rubber Band-Powered Boat

3. Drive system: Get 2 dowels, each about 6 inches long. When the boat hull is ready, tape each dowel to the outside of boat, one on each side. The dowels need to be close to the bottom of the boat so the paddle will be in the water. Extend the dowels at least 2 inches behind the boat so you'll be able to attach the propeller.

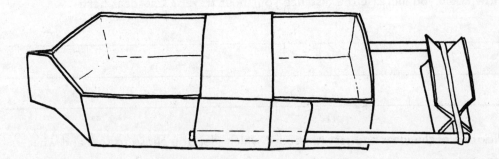

The stern-wheel version of the rubber band–powered boat fits into a 6-inch wide trough for testing. The duct tape holds the sides in place, opposing the pull of the rubber band on the propeller.

4. Loop a rubber band onto the propeller. Loop one end onto one dowel and the other end onto the other dowel.

5. To power the rubber band motor, wind the propeller. Think about which direction you want the boat to travel and which direction you need to wind the propeller to make the boat move in that direction. When you have wound the propeller so the rubber band is fairly tight, release it with the boat in the water.

Name: _____

# Rubber Band-Powered Boat

## TEST

How far will your boat go? What can you do to make it travel farther? Measure the distance and record it below.

## TOY INVENTOR'S LOG

Measure how far your boat travels. Distance _____ (units) _____

How could you increase the distance your boat travels? List ideas here.

1. _____

2. _____

3. _____

Pick one of the ideas and test it. Record which idea you chose to test and what happened.

_____

_____

_____

Test your boat again and record how many times you rotate the propeller and how far the boat travels. This number of rotations will serve as the maximum number.

Number of times you rotate the propeller: _____

Distance _____ (units)_____

Test your boat again, winding the propeller fewer times as indicated below.

Number of rotations = 75 percent of maximum = _____number of turns.

Distance _____ (units) _____

Number of rotations = 50 percent of maximum = _____number of turns.

Distance _____ (units) _____

Number of rotations = 25 percent of maximum = _____number of turns.

Distance _____ (units) _____

# Rubber Band-Powered Boat

Each time you rotate the propeller, you store energy in the rubber band. The greater the number of rotations, the more energy the boat will have. From the experiment you just ran, what can you say about how the number of rotations of the rubber band affects how far the boat travels?

————————————————————————————————————

## REFLECT

In this activity you used rubber bands to store energy. Metal springs are often used to store energy. Where do you see metal or elastic springs used?

# Diving Submarine

## Challenge

Make a submarine that dives when you apply pressure to its container.

## Overview

This is a great activity to get kids thinking about buoyancy and pressure. Each student can make his or her own submarine in a bottle or teams can work together.

## Materials

> 2-liter bottles with lids (1 per team or per student)
> Condiment packets from fast-food restaurants
> Paper clips, large and small
> Water

## Design Concept

This is a simple version of a Cartesian diver. Squeezing a water-filled two-liter bottle causes the condiment packet to sink. Releasing pressure allows it to rise.

## The Details

The trick is to get a condiment packet to be almost neutrally buoyant. Add a paper clip and test it. Keep adding paper clips until the packet floats before you squeeze the bottle. You may have to trim some metal off a paper clip (using a wire cutter) to get the exact weight you need. Put the submarine (packet) in the bottle and completely fill the bottle. Cap it tightly.

## Getting Started

Demonstrate your finished submarine in the bottle to the class. Hold it up and invite a student to come forward and be the submarine's captain. Ask the student to hold one hand horizontally, adjacent to the floating packet. Direct the student to slowly lower

A condiment packet, weighted to have an only slightly positive buoyancy, sinks when you squeeze the water-filled bottle.

the hand and, as the hand lowers, squeeze the bottle. Mysteriously the packet will sink as the hand lowers. Have the student raise and lower the hand several times, as you squeeze and release the bottle in sync with the hand motion.

Without explanation, invite teams or individuals to make their own diving submarine. Allow them to see your model and then construct their own.

## Teachable Moments

Challenge students to figure out why the submarine rises and falls. Someone will see your hand tighten and suggest that you are making it happen. Once the students realize that there is an air bubble in the packet, illustrate on the board how the tiny air bubble keeps the packet afloat. Increasing the pressure by squeezing the bottle causes this air bubble to shrink. Gases take up less volume under pressure. With a smaller volume of air supporting the packet, it sinks. Releasing the pressure allows the air bubble to expand to its original size and the packet floats to the top.

This activity also demonstrates that pressure is uniform throughout a liquid. You squeeze on the sides of the bottle to raise the pressure everywhere inside it.

Also, this activity demonstrates that unlike air, water is incompressible. Although squeezing the bottle causes the air bubble to shrink, the water volume doesn't change noticeably. A water-filled balloon would have (almost) the same dimensions at the surface of the ocean as at the bottom. However, an air-filled balloon shrinks to a fraction of its surface size when just one hundred meters underwater.

Name: _____

# Diving Submarine

## CHALLENGE

Control the vertical movements of a submarine inside a plastic bottle by increasing the pressure inside the bottle.

## DESIGN

Sketch the inside of the condiment packet, showing the relative size of the air bubble in two cases: when the packet is at the top of the bottle and when it is at the bottom.

Packet at the top

Packet at the bottom

## TEST

Demonstrate that you can make your submarine sink and rise by squeezing the bottle.

# Diving Submarine

## EXTEND

How do real submarines sink and rise in the water? (If you don't know, research submarines in an encyclopedia or at one of these "how things work" Web sites:

http://science.howstuffworks.com/submarine.htm

http://www.onr.navy.mil/focus/blowballast/sub/work2.htm

In your own words, describe how submarines work:

_____

_____

_____

_____

_____

_____

# Bibliography

Balmer, Al. *Mouse Trap Cars: A Teacher's Guide*. Round Rock, Texas: Doc Fizzix Publishing Company, 1998.

Sobey, Ed. *Young Inventors at Work: Learning Science by Doing Science*. Glenview, Illinois: Good Year Books, 1999.

———. *Fantastic Flying Fun with Science*. New York: McGraw-Hill, 2000.

———. *Wacky Water Fun with Science*. New York: McGraw-Hill, 2000.

———. *Inventing Toys: Kids Having Fun Learning Science*. Tucson: Zephyr Press, 2002.

Walker, Jearl. *The Flying Circus of Physics with Answers*. New York: John Wiley & Sons, 1977.

After nearly twenty years directing museums, Ed Sobey created the Northwest Invention Center to serve schools and museums with hands-on programs and exhibits and to help inventors. The Center creates exhibits for museums in the United States, Europe, and Asia. Ed also originated and hosted a television show on inventing and co-hosted a science series for Ohio Public Broadcast Network. He holds a Ph.D. in oceanography from Oregon State University and taught museum management at the University of Washington. Ed founded the National Toy Hall of Fame and has written more than a dozen books including *Inventing Toys*, *Inventing Stuff*, and *How to Win Invention Contests*, and other books on subjects from backpacking to robots and kids' science projects. Ed is a Fellow of the Explorers Club and chairs its Pacific Northwest Chapter.